THE 50s 50s 50s

DESIGNING
America's
CARS

FROM DRAWING BOARD TO DRIVEWAY

pil

Publications International, Ltd.

Louis Weber, CEO
Publications International, Ltd.
7373 North Cicero Avenue
Lincolnwood, Illinois 60712

Permission is never granted for commercial purposes.

Manufactured in China.

8 7 6 5 4 3 2 1

ISBN: 1-4127-1157-6

Library of Congress Control Number: 2004115107

Acknowledgements

PHOTOGRAPHY
The editors gratefully acknowledge those who supplied photography and other resources that helped make this book possible:

Roger D. Barnes; Scott Baxter; Ken Beebe; Buick Division of GM; Robert Burrington; Cadillac Division of GM; Chevrolet Division of GM; Chrysler Historical Collection; Randy Edmonds; Al Ferreira; Ford Motor Company; Jim Frenak; Nina Fuller; Russ Garrett; Thomas Glatch; GM Photographic; Jeff Godshall; Eddie Goldberger; Gary Greene; Sam Griffith; Jerry Heasley; Don Heiny; Hutchinson Photo; David Jensen; Bud Juneau; Laurel H. Kenney; Milton Kieft; Lloyd Koening; Rick Lenz; Randy Lorentzen; Dan Lyons; Vince Manocchi; Ron McQueeney; Doug Mitchel; Ron Moorhead; Mike Mueller; The National Automotive Historical Collection-Detroit Public Library; David Newhardt; Eddie Noggles; Oldsmobile Division of GM; Nina Padgett-Russin; David Patryas; Pontiac Division of GM; Richard Quinn; Larry & Alice Richter; Jeff Rose; Bill Schintz; Tom Shaw; Gary Smith; Mike Spenner; Richard Spiegelman; David Temple; Bob Tenney; Marvin Terrell; Phil Toy; Ross Tse; Dan Vecchio; W. C. Waymack; Nicky Wright.

ILLUSTRATION
Paul W. Gillan; R. H. Gurr; Ronald C. Hill; Robin Jones; Frank Peiler; Larry Shinoda; Brooks Stevens.

OWNERS
Special thanks to the owners of the cars featured in this book for their enthusiastic cooperation. They are listed below:

Bobo Aaron; Chuck & Laurie Abbot; Mervin M. Afflerbach; Andrew Alphonso; Barbara Ann; Christopher Antal; Len Antrim; Mark Apel; Gordon Apker; Art Astor; Kurt & Connie Atkinson; Edward Bagdonas; John Baker; Edward Ballenger; Tom & Karen Barnes; Charles Beed; Richard & Maureen Beggs; Steve Bergin; Michael Berzenye; Neil S. Black; Gary Blakeslee; Jim Blanchard; Frank R. Bobek; Leeland V. Bortmas; Milt McMillen & Paul Brieske; Bill Bruce; Joseph Bua; Dale M. Bunsen; William Burgun; Winton & Kitty Burns; Butch's Rod Shop; Jerry Capizzi/Cappy Collection®; Gerry Capp; Bonnie Carey; Joe Carfagna; Ken Carmack; Richard Carpenter/ Yesterday Once More, Ltd.; Dick Choler; Lauretta Chromicz; Jerry Cinotti; John Clark; Dave Comstock; Dan Coughlin; David Cutler; Ted Dahlmann; Arthur & Suzanne Dalby; Richard Daly; Edward & Joanne Dauer; Jim Davidson; Beau Day; Deer Park Car Museum; Hank Deglman; Tom Devers; Jim DiGregorio; James Dowdy; Stanley & Phyllis Dumes; Paul Eggerling; Lee Eichmann; Clifford L. Elmore; Bob Elwood; James Emmi; Galen & Fay Erb; Fairway Chevrolet; David Ferguson; Jim Ferrero; Don & Barb Finn; Hudson Firestone;

Norm Frey; Howard Funck; John Galandak; Kenneth Geiger; Ken Gimelli; David Goetz; Clark Goodwin; Tim Graves; James Greene; Jim D. Gregoria; David L. Griebling; Greg Gustafson; Jerry & Barb Guthrie; Mario Gutierrez; Tim & Sharon Hacker; Bernie Hackett; Ron Hagen; Bill & Anna Harper; Ralph Harstock; Carl Herren; Dave Higby; Garth Higgins; Bud Hiler; Ten Hinkle; Rick Holmes; Joe Holler; Alan Hoff; Jeff Alexander & Scott Holloran; Art & Vicky Hoock; David Horn; Dick Hoyt; Bill Hubert; Virgil Hudkins; Dennis Huff; Bill & Margaret Hunter; Gary L. Ingersoll; Fred & Diane Ives; Howard Johnston; Aaron Kahlenberg; Sherwood Kahlenberg; Arnold Kaplan; Thomas Karkiewicz; John Keck; Gene Keepes; Jerry Keller; Austin Kelley; Brian Kelly; Royce & Clydette Kidd; Barton Kogan; Ron & Donna Krauss; Don Kreider; Andrew Krizman; Philip Kuhn; David & Anne Kurtz; Wayne & Pat Lasley; William Lawler; Donald Lawson; Aivar Lejins; Richard Lesson; Richard L. Leu; Dorsey Lewis; Ken Lindsey; William R. Lindsey; Art Lostumo, Jr.; Frank Lyle; Bill & Rita Malik; Larry Martin; Neil Martin/ Goldenrod Garage; Richard Matsun; Jack & Jan Matske; Robert & Charlene Matteoli; Roy & Bonnie McClain; Gary McClaine; Al McCormick; Dave & Barb McCoy; Steve Megyesi; Gary Mills; George Mills; Amos Minter; Dennis B. Miracky; Michael J. Morelli; Guy Morice; Gary Morrison; Milt Mouser; Donald Muchmore; Jim Mueller; Robert Muench; Rick Mullen; John L. Murray; Dick Nelson; Tom Null; Frank Oatman; Ed Oberhaus; Ray Ostrander; Dennis Pagliano; John Parker; Glen & Barbara Patch; Bob Schmidt & Glen Patch; Bob Patrick; Henry Patrick; Robert Perez; Marshall & Ellie Peters; John Petras; Joseph Piccione; Bob Porter; Michael Porto; Joel Prescott; Richard Presson; Bob Strous & Lizzie Pusch; Glen & Janice Pykiet; Glen & Vera Reints; Wayne Rife; Jerry Robbin; Cliff & Sandy Roberts; Hank Roeter; Bob Rose; Art & Jared Rosen; Glyn-Jan Rowley; Charles Rublaitus; Jess Ruffalo; Al & Alice Russell; Arthur Sabin; John Sanders; John Sobers & Bruce Sansone; Al Schaefer; Bob Schlenk; William & Joseph Schoenbeck; Bill Schwelitz; John Scopelite; Robert N. Seiple; Rosemary & Duane Sell; Tom Shafer; Bob & Roni Sue Shapiro; James & John Sharp; J. W. Silviera; Mary & Marshall Simpkin; Walter Smith; Don & Wanda Spivey; Bill & Colette Stanley; Michael J. Stecco; Charles Stinnett; David Stipp; Davis A. Studer; Neil Sugg; Tom Taylor; Gary Thomas; Ken & Esther Thompson; June Trombley; Tom Turner; Joel Twainten; Dean Ullman; James & Susan Verhasselt; John R. Vorva; Jeff Wade; Ron Wakefield; Donald Walkemeyer; Jeff Walther; Charles & Charlotte Watons; George Watts; Wayne Davis Restoration; Glen Weeks; Herbert Wehling; Jeff & Aleta Wells; George Wenk; Dann Whalen; Dave Williamson/Community Trading Center; Thomas Witt; John Wood; Frank E. Wrenick; Charles & Veronica Wurm; Dennis Yauger; Ron Yori; Roy Yost; Mearl Zeigler; Richard Zeigler.

CONTENTS

FOREWORD

Americans have always been proud of their cars. They have cherished the sense of personal freedom and mobility an automobile provides, and they've basked in the boost of status (and just maybe a bit of the neighbors' envy) that comes with taking the keys to one fresh off the showroom floor. Should a vote be held to select a national scent, "that new-car smell" would rank right up there with a freshly baked apple pie for a lot of Americans.

If ever there was a time when this sense of pride might have bordered on being something more—love, perhaps?—it certainly would have been in the Fifties. These were the years when car dealers papered over their showroom windows every autumn to receive the new models, then pulled down the sheets on introduction day as if unveiling a new work of art to a rapt public. They were the years when owners of that other great status symbol of the day—a television set—could hear Dinah Shore sing the praises of Chevrolets, or visit their DeSoto dealer and "tell him Groucho sent you."

Consumers who heeded the siren call to dis-cover what awaited behind the covered windows were treated to their share of technical advances.

High-compression ohv V-8 engines, fully automatic transmissions, and air conditioning—all of which had gotten a toehold in the Forties—gained wider acceptance. There were new suspension systems and a host of power-assisted conveniences available, too. But what really made jaws drop was the part that the customers could see: the styling.

Fifties American cars reached unprecedented levels of imagination and daring (even audacity, perhaps) in their appearance. There were "upside-down bathtubs"; envelope bodies; dramatic, if impractical, wraparound windshields; artillery-shell "Dagmar" bumpers; a riot of color in two- and even three-tone combinations; fake wood; real chrome—lots of it; and, of course, tailfins. From year to year and brand to brand, it all put on a dazzling show during the decade.

By the Fifties, the U.S. auto industry had long recognized the emotional attachment its customers had for its products. Early in the automobile age,

6

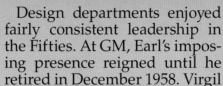

manufacturers stressed the mechanical competence of their vehicles. Then, when it became clear that everyone in the business could make a car that would reliably start, go, and stop, something else would be required to differentiate one brand from another. Enter the stylist.

General Motors was the first American automaker to recognize that appearances might count in the contest for sales. GM turned to Californian Harley J. Earl—who already had experience individualizing cars for the wealthy—to establish an "Art & Colour Section" in the late Twenties.

It took a while before Earl could get control of the body-design process—some engineers felt it was their job—but the success of his staff's efforts eventually won respect for the role of the stylist. Rival carmakers ignored styling at their own peril; soon they were forming their own styling shops or contracting with outside designers.

Design departments enjoyed fairly consistent leadership in the Fifties. At GM, Earl's imposing presence reigned until he retired in December 1958. Virgil Exner, hired by Chrysler in 1949 to do advanced designs, became styling director in 1953. Ford made George Walker its first vice president of styling in 1955, but he had been involved in Dearborn's designs as a consultant since the late Forties. Ed Anderson set up Nash's first in-house styling group in 1950, then continued in the top spot after the 1954 merger with Hudson that created American Motors Corporation. Raymond Loewy's longtime contract with Studebaker ran out in 1955, but even then the cars that followed through the rest of the decade were derived from designs done by his staff. Still, styling cars for mass producers was not a solitary pursuit. It took teams of designers and clay modelers to conceive, shape, and revise the designs that would win approval to go into production.

Designing America's Cars, the '50s: From Drawing Board to Driveway singles out a number of the personalities behind the cars of the Fifties that remain enthusiast favorites today. Each company had its own approach to styling. Jeffrey Godshall brings his experience as a professional car designer and automotive historian to bear in essays that open this book's eight manufacturer sections, highlighting the themes, the successes, and the failures associated with those companies. Finally, the editors of *Collectible Automobile®* magazine have compiled a group of intriguing behind-the-scenes sketches and photos that reveal the scope of imagination—some weird and some wonderful—that flowed through America's car design studios in the Fifties.

AMERICAN MOTORS CORPORATION

Maybe they were destined for each other: Hudson and Nash—the companies that would merge to form American Motors in 1954—both entered the Fifties with radical postwar streamliners, each using a unitized body. The "Stepdown" Hudson was the better looking, with relatively taut surfaces and a hunkered-down look that foretold the stock-car racing victories that lay just ahead with the Twin H-Power Hornets.

Looking much like the postwar automobile prophesized in countless Sunday newspaper supplements during World War II, the Nash "Airflyte" was a rotund design with roly-poly surfaces. Much of the look was dictated by Nash-Kelvinator's equally rotund president, George Mason, and company engineering director Nils Erik Wahlberg. With all wheels buried beneath the smoothed sheetmetal, the "wheelless" Airflyte looked aerodynamic and it was. Wind tunnel tests held at the University of Wichita confirmed that Nash was the "slipperiest" car in America with a .429 coefficient of drag. Despite its ungainly look and huge turning radius, the Airflyte sold well.

But Nash's big news in 1950 was the new Rambler, America's first successful compact. In appearance a virtual twin of the bigger Statesman and Ambassador, the Rambler was a risky undertaking, a niche vehicle that Mason hoped would give Nash a marketing edge. Introduced first as a convertible, then a wagon and a hardtop (all two-doors), there wasn't a bread-and-butter four-door sedan in the line until 1954. But by bringing out the more expensive body styles first, and equipping them generously, Nash was able to avoid having the Rambler perceived as a "cheap" car. It was a product coup that would save the company.

Mason's product-planning initiatives didn't end with the Rambler. By 1954, Nash was offering the even smaller two-seat Metropolitan, designed by William Flajole. Patterned off the earlier NXI show car and built by Austin of England, almost 95,000 "Mets" would find customers before sales ended in 1962. Another of Mason's inventive transatlantic efforts was the attractive Nash-Healey sports car produced from 1951 to 1954.

Former General Motors designer Ed Anderson was hired in 1950 to establish Nash's first corporate styling studio. When Anderson's team redid the big Nash for '52 and the Rambler a year later, the cars—though still "wheelless"—were crisper, "three-box" designs with the hoods sunk beneath the fenders. Their chaste flanks bore the crest of Italian designer Pinin Farina, hired by Mason as a consultant. Although Anderson's team did most of the design work, publicity reasons dictated that Farina got the credit. About this time Nash began featuring "continental" tire kits as a styling cue, which rendered the cars even less maneuverable.

The nicest-looking Fifties Nash was the '55, with its distinctive grille-mounted headlights lifted from the Nash-Healey. Although the '56s and '57s were disfigured by haphazard bodyside two-toning, the 1957 Nash shared the distinction (with the Cadillac Eldorado Brougham) as the first U.S. car with standard quad headlights.

The Hornet and its racing victories kept Hudson in the running as company president A. E. Barit championed the firm's new products. The radical Italia sports coupe, designed by Hudson styling chief Frank Spring, was a car that could have served as the basis for future Hornets and Wasps. However, Barit bet much of Hudson's scarce capital on the compact 1953-54 Jet. Unfortunately for Hudson, the narrow, awkward-looking Jet was no Rambler. Its failure led Barit, hat in hand, to Mason, who had long envisioned bringing the four largest remaining independent automakers under one umbrella. The Nash-based '55 Hudson was tolerable from an appearance standpoint (though anathema to Hudson diehards), but Richard Arbib's "V-line" '56 facelift and its '57 successor were truly bizarre. By 1958, both the venerable Nash and Hudson names were gone.

When George Mason died suddenly in October 1954, he was succeeded by George Romney, who had been earlier recruited by Mason as his successor. Romney believed in the compact car with an almost religious passion. A major redesign of the Rambler in 1956 gave America its first four-door hardtop station wagon, but the "Safety Arch" three-toning proved controversial and was modified midyear on the sedans. By 1958, Ramblers were sporting modest tailfins, even though Romney was busily caricaturing rivals' finned full-size cars as "dinosaurs" in magazine advertisements.

Romney would prove nearly as resourceful as Mason, resurrecting the 100-inch-wheelbase '55 Rambler tooling and astonishing the industry by putting the car back in production in the spring of 1958 as the American. Though the basic body design dated back to 1953, the car sold well despite the styling anomaly of a square wheel opening up front and a teardrop-shaped wheel opening in the rear.

Given the circumstances, concentrating on small cars was the right decision. As the Fifties closed, AMC was about to enter its golden years.

1-2. The decision to build 1955-57 Hudsons on the Nash body was driven by the economics of the moment, but it resulted in smaller Hudsons. These drawings from 1955 envisioned a '57 Hudson on a 125-inch wheelbase more akin to the marque's premerger size. **3-4.** A Hudson logo graces the front of this design model. **5-6.** Added "V" motifs on the front and tacked-on tailfins marked actual 1957 Hudsons.

Hudson made it through the first half of the Fifties with cosmetic updates of its 1948-vintage "Step-down" model. The road-hugging car's unitized construction melded Stuart Baits's engineering principles with Frank Spring's styling ideas.

Then, on May 1, 1954, Hudson merged with Nash to form American Motors, and it was decided that future Hudsons would share Nash bodies. "Hudsonized" versions of the Nash were made from 1955 to 1957, but for a time, a return to a more-distinctive Hudson was on the drawing board.

5

6

As American Motors Corporation began planning for the 1958 model year, it fully intended to produce Nash and Hudson cars. However, a last-minute decision ended those plans and consigned both nameplates to automotive history.

Slow sales of the "Hash" —a derisive term for the Hudson/Nash vehicles— convinced AMC Chairman George Romney to place the company's emphasis on the 108-inch-wheelbase Rambler. Still, there would be Hudsons and Nashes on a stretched version of the '58 Rambler platform.

The trim and grille workouts for both brands were devised. Then, in mid 1957, financial considerations led Romney to fold them into a single big Rambler.

1. Vertical quad headlamps, which AMC had already used on the 1957 Nash, were considered for the presumptive '58 Hudson. 2-5. Several styling models of the developing long-wheelbase Rambler sedan and wagon bodies wore Hudson badges. 6. Standing, from left, assistant styling director Bill Reddig, styling director Edmund Anderson, and AMC Chairman George Romney observe a stylist's work in the mid Fifties. 7-9. Another possibility for a post-1957 Hudson was this finny sedan with hints of the "V-Line" theme used on 1956-57 production cars.

1952 NASH

1

Nash-Kelvinator Chairman George Mason was a busy man as 1950 dawned. Not only was he still pursuing his dream of a merger of independent automakers, but he was bringing out new products and starting the company's first in-house auto styling team.

Ex-General Motors designer Edmund Anderson was hired to select and direct the group. Its first task: Come up with a design for the Ambassador and Statesman for 1952, which would be the company's 50th anniversary. However, the firm had also signed noted Italian designer Pinin Farina to do likewise. Ultimately, Farina touches were added to what was basically a Nash design.

1. This flight of fancy from Bill Reddig, one of the first Nash stylists, incorporates the high-fenderline/low-hood look of the company's early Fifties cars. **2.** An early rendering includes versions of final production details for '52, such as a grille of thick vertical teeth and a grooved beltline indentation atop the doors. **3-6.** Scale models for a four-door sedan (3-4) and two-door hardtop (5-6). Engineering chief Nils Wahlberg advocated skirted wheel openings for their aerodynamics.

2

3

4

5

6

1

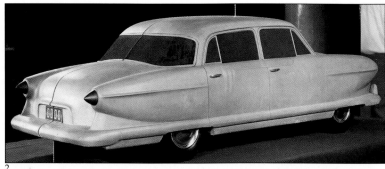

2

3

1-5. Models and a full-size drawing show proposed design details. A boatlike profile (1-2) was rejected for a smoother look. **6-7.** Nash managers preferred the car their stylists had designed for 1952, but found it wise from a publicity standpoint to incorporate some of Pinin Farina's ideas and attribute the car's design to the Italian. A reverse-angle rear-roof pillar was one of the changes made. The Statesman was the smaller of the two senior Nash lines.

4

5

6

7

1 9 5 5   N A S H

After three years on the market with slight changes, the 1952-vintage Nash design was ready for a new look for 1955. The company did not have the wherewithal for a top-to-bottom new body, but Ed Anderson's

1

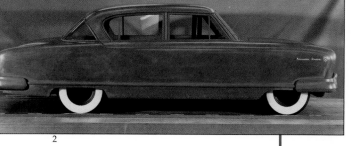

2

3

stylists considerably freshened the existing shells.

Great changes were seen up front. Headlamps moved inboard to an oval grille, and forward-canted fender blades held vertical parking lights. The grille and fenders were inspired by the Farina-styled Nash-Healey sports car of 1952-54.

Nash gained a wraparound windshield with vertical A-pillars, per the trends of 1955. Upper-door sheetmetal was smoothed out and front wheel openings were slightly enlarged.

4

5

1-5. Design models from 1953 display different ideas about rear-fender styling. The "dogleg" A-pillar had not yet been added. **6.** New front fenders were conducive to trendy two-tone paintwork, such as seen on this 1955 Statesman two-door hardtop. **7.** Pinin Farina used a '55 Ambassador to create this prototype for a possible late-Fifties Nash/Hudson design.

6

7

1957 NASH

When the 1957 Nash was introduced, no one knew it would be the last to bear a name that had been around for 40 years. As the '57 was going on sale, AMC executives were looking ahead to a new model for 1958 and beyond.

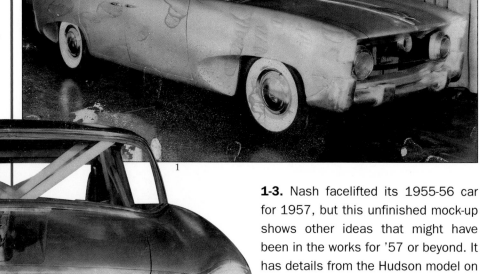

1-3. Nash facelifted its 1955-56 car for 1957, but this unfinished mock-up shows other ideas that might have been in the works for '57 or beyond. It has details from the Hudson model on page 10 (roof and fender coves), and its front has some of the look of the Farina concept on page 19. **4-7.** Fully open front wheels, a revised grille, and quad headlamps marked Ambassador Customs (4-5) and Supers (6-7).

After the Nash-Hudson merger created American Motors, Edmund Anderson was named styling director for the corporation. Though his department was fairly small, Anderson set up specific studios. Jack Garnier was put in charge of Nash styling in 1955.

The 1957 facelift of the 1955 update of the '52 body centered on stacked quad headlights and a new grille.

4

5

6

7

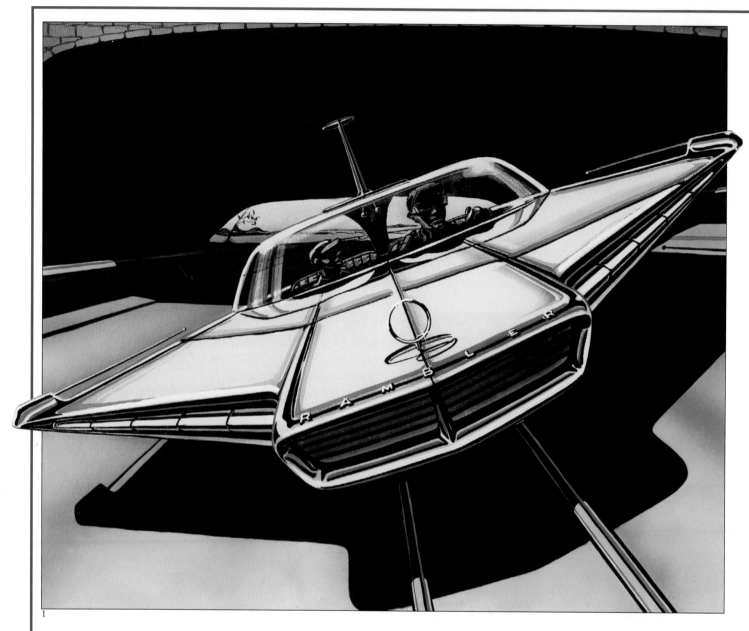

1

For the American auto industry, the Rambler was proof of the idea that from small things great things one day come. Nash Chairman George Mason brought out the Rambler in 1950 as a well-equipped compact adjunct to his firm's standard cars. After Mason's death in 1954, his successor, George Romney, viewed the Rambler as the key to the future of what was now American Motors. By 1958, the Rambler was AMC's sole homegrown automotive line.

Romney got styling director Ed Anderson to speed up work on the planned '57 Rambler. The fresh, successful design arrived for 1956.

1. A fanciful rendering from Bill Reddig. The Rambler *was* the future for AMC. **2.** The developing 1956 Rambler design as it appeared in '55. Grille mesh, parking lights, and side trim would all be changed by the start of production. **3.** Bladelike tailfins would have to wait for later Ramblers. **4.** The taillamp treatment at left was picked for production; the slanted retractable rear window was not—though a working prototype was made. **5.** A studio for advanced design gave freer rein to stylists' notions.

1. For the '56 Rambler, the mesh grille idea was dropped in favor of an enlarged eggcrate look. Nash's familiar grille-and-headlamp motif was retained. Parking lights were sited below the curve of the fendertops, and were neither enormous nor peculiarly heavy-lidded. Single-color Customs featured irregular side trim. **2.** Trim on the plain-Jane but pleasing Super sedan paralleled the flow of the belt-line into the roof C-pillar. **3-4.** The Custom four-door hardtop retained the rakish pillarless design of early studies. Although some concepts had prominent tailfins, Rambler resisted the trend, at least for the moment, with appealingly rounded rear fendertops. Bodyside trim on tri-toned cars was aggressive, though.

1

3

2

24

1959 RAMBLER

When Rambler was made the focus of AMC carmaking plans in the mid Fifties, it became crucial to keep it modern and competitive. Thus, the 1956-57 Rambler, with its "basket-handle" roof and scaled-down Nash looks wasn't going to be allowed to grow too long in the tooth.

An all-new body for 1958 was out of the question, but corporate stylists so

drastically redid the sheetmetal that it seemed new. Actually, the '58 Rambler adopted a period Detroit look, with a broad grille/parking-light ensemble, hooded quad headlamps set above the grille, and flaring tailfins.

The facelifted '59 Rambler sported revised side trim and a new grille. Tops of the restyled rear doors gained a "kickup" effect that flowed smoothly into the fins, making the cars look longer.

4

5

1. This two-side styling mock-up (note the sedan B-pillar on the far side) photographed in 1958 still has a tailfin that terminates just behind the rear door, as was used on production '58 Ramblers. **2-5.** Other cars in the studio being evaluated for possible trim packages show how the tops of the rear doors were modified to form an unbroken line along the beltline to the fins. This feature was adopted for the '59 model year.

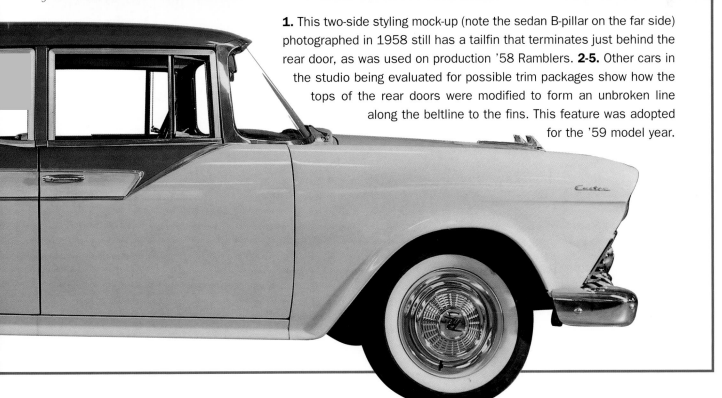

1

3

2

1-2. The '59 Ramblers, including this Six Custom four-door sedan, are among the most interesting and uniquely styled American cars of the Fifties. Although distinctive in the extreme, they arguably suffered from a visual identity crisis. The familiar Nash front end had evolved into extinction, and although quad headlamps and canted tailfins picked up on trends of the moment, Rambler's tall greenhouse and very high deck made the whole package look chunky and stubby. Here is where AMC's tight finances really hurt, because radically tweaked sheetmetal could not compensate for an old body that badly needed to be replaced. **3.** The reshaped rear doors added some visual punch; a gently curved kickup created an unbroken line from the headlight caps to the fin tips.

AMBASSADOR

N ot all the work that went into the idea of keeping the Nash and Hudson alive for 1958 went for naught when George Romney decided to cancel those cars. A single long-wheelbase version of the '58 Rambler was devised and given the Ambassador name that had been used by Nash for 30 years.

All the Ambassador's extra length was ahead of the firewall. The grille, side trim, and wheel covers lent visual distinction to the Ambassador.

1-2. Long front fenders on these Rambler-badged clays from 1956 indicate intent to build a larger version of the car already under consideration for the 108-inch-wheelbase platform. 3. The grille and parking lights from this proposed Nash design were adopted for '58. The grille "V" was replaced by a similarly shaped bumper guard from the Hudson workup seen on page 12. 4-5. Rejected side-trim ideas for '59 offered a choice of paint (4) or annodized metal (5).

2

3

5

Stretched-wheelbase concepts that had been planned as Hudsons and Nashes were amalgamated under the name Ambassador to form Rambler's new flagship line. **1-3.** The 1958 Custom Cross Country hardtop wagon had the length needed to justify the design's busier aspects; it was clearly a modern car, with dramatically shaped side windows and fins that seemed comfortable with the bodyshell. **4-5.** Ed Anderson's design team struck gold with the beautifully proportioned, pillar-less Custom Country Club, which was facelifted for '59.

1

2

3

4

5

CHRYSLER CORPORATION

The essential point about Chrysler styling in the Fifties is this: The company entered the decade with cars designed by engineers and exited it with its cars designed by stylists.

"Bigger on the inside, smaller on the outside," Chrysler's all-new—but conservative—1949 models reflected the priorities of its pragmatic and well-respected engineering staff. Those priorties meshed well with the personal taste of the company's president, K. T. Keller, who apparently always drove wearing his legendary hat. Conventional as they were, as the '49 designs matured through 1952, they were not without their styling innovations; to wit, the combination bumper/grille on the 1951-53 Imperials and the "grilleless" 1951 and '52 Chryslers with deep-set body-color air intakes supplanting the customary chrome fencing. Buttressed with solid engineering innovations like hemispherical V-8s and power steering, the company's cars sold just well enough for Chrysler to continue to believe that the American public bought automobiles solely on some kind of rational basis.

This assumption led the company to further shrink its high-volume Plymouth and Dodge models in 1953, with Dodge's "glamour cars"—the hardtop, convertible, and station wagon—sharing Plymouth's 114-inch wheelbase. At a time when American cars were growing larger, this was a major marketing blunder. All the chickens came home to roost in 1954, when Chrysler's market share plummeted as its clumsily facelifted cars were bested by sharp-looking new Buicks and Oldsmobiles. If Chrysler was to avoid further humiliation, it needed a savior.

Providentially, K. T. had provided for such a man back in 1949, when he lured the talented Virgil Exner from Studebaker. At first, Exner was confined to creating a spate of innovative "idea cars" like the K-310, D'Elegance, Flight Sweep I and II, and the handsome Falcon roadster. But in 1953, his apprenticeship over, "Ex" was made director of styling and given full responsibility for the corporation's all-new cars for 1955.

Christened "The Forward Look" by Chrysler's ad agency, Exner's new line of longer, lower, and more colorful automobiles (some with tri-tones) brought the company at least even with the competition. The majestic Imperial benefited from K-310 cues like fully circular wheel openings and freestanding "microphone" taillights. The year also saw the first of the famed 300s, the "executive hot rod" whose magic still lives today.

The following year, Chrysler became the first company to affix fins on every one of its passenger cars for a high-in-back, low-in-front wedge silhouette. Exner believed that the wedge—as typified by the jaunty profiles of jet aircraft and Gold Cup speedboats—was the essence of motion.

But the fins of 1956 were modest compared to what came next. Backed to the hilt by Chrysler president L. L. "Tex" Colbert, Exner's all-new 1957 cars took fins to new heights, both figuratively and literally. The new vehicles were simply stunning, even in advertisements. A two-page *Life* magazine ad headlined "Suddenly, it's 1960!" depicted a jaw-dropping, gold-colored, two-door hardtop with uplifted rudder tailfins and a seemingly handkerchief-sized roof supported by the thinest pillars imaginable. And that was just the Plymouth! The Dodge, DeSoto, and Chrysler were equally spectacular. Especially dramatic was the new Imperial, with its long, gracefully finned quarters, "Flight Sweep" decklid (another K-310 idea), and flowing rooflines featuring a compound-curve windshield and curved side glass, each a first for an American car.

The front ends were also inventive, from Dodge's bold bumper-bar grille to DeSoto's bumper-over-grille combo and the overpowering trapezoidal grille on the 300, a favorite cue from Exner's "idea cars."

Exner's finned fantasies established Chrysler as the industry's styling champion overnight, to the chagrin of the accustomed leader, General Motors.

Adding insult to injury, Chrysler took a leaf out of Fisher Body's interchangeability bag of tricks. Each of Chrysler's new cars (save Imperial) shared the same basic body and expensive-to-tool cowl structure, saving millions. This also enabled the company to utilize a common shell for all its station wagons, from the lowly Plymouth Deluxe Suburban to the ritzy Chrysler New Yorker Town & Country, by simply bolting on different marque-specific front-end clips and adding the appropriate side trim, taillights, and instrument panels.

The dazzled public responded with a flood of orders. By year's end, Chrysler had nearly met its goal of 20 percent market share, and Exner was rewarded with a vice presidency, the first ever for a Chrysler stylist. But build-quality problems disillusioned many owners, and the facelifted '58s and '59s were not as attractive as the '57s. Moreover, the corporate image was now tied to fins. Raising them to any extent was impractical, but removing them would invariably look like a retreat. This thorny and self-created problem would confound Exner's styling team as it moved into the Sixties.

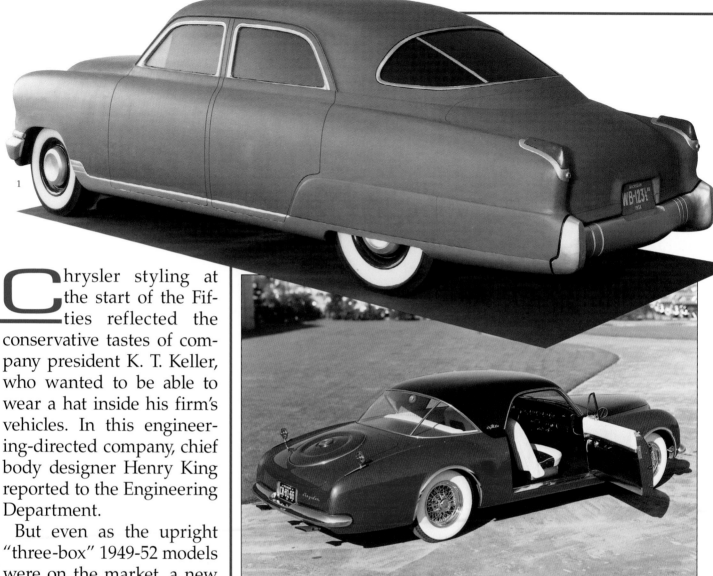

Chrysler styling at the start of the Fifties reflected the conservative tastes of company president K. T. Keller, who wanted to be able to wear a hat inside his firm's vehicles. In this engineering-directed company, chief body designer Henry King reported to the Engineering Department.

But even as the upright "three-box" 1949-52 models were on the market, a new die was being cast for Chrysler's styling future. Virgil Exner, late of Studebaker, was hired in '49 to head an advanced-design studio. The new president installed in late 1950, L. L. "Tex" Colbert, favored more-stylish cars. He eventually promoted Exner, who had a chance to exert some influence on the rebodied 1953-54 Chryslers.

1-2. Nash-like models from late 1948 were studies for possible early Fifties Chryslers. **3.** From '51, top-line Imperials had their own frontal styling. This December 1952 workup for the '54s was rejected. **4-7.** Ghia-built Virgil Exner advanced designs like the K-310 (4-5), D'Elegance (6), and C-200 (7) previewed upcoming production-car details.

1. The wood-trimmed Town & Country picked up a hardtop for 1950, but the convertible went away. A three-piece wraparound backlight, called the "clearbac," was shared with other Chrysler hardtops. 2. The 1951 New Yorker was softened overall, but the nose treatment remained heavy. 3. The '51 T & C wagon was almost stately. 4. The 1952 Imperial served notice that the "three-box" look was fading. 5-6. For '53, Virgil Exner virtually eliminated separate rear fenders, as on the New Yorker and Custom Imperial. 7-8. Note the graceful grille of the '54 New Yorker DeLuxe convertible. 9. Meanwhile, Custom Imperials adopted a far simpler grille for 1954.

5

6

7

8

9

Virgil Exner got his first chance to design a line of cars according to his sensibilities for the 1955 model year. The result was the "Forward Look."

At first, Exner tried to use the K-310 "idea car" as the basis for the 1955 Chrysler and Imperial—the latter of which was to be marketed as a separate make for the first time. When that proved to be unworkable, he turned to one of his advanced studio projects—a long-wheelbase dual-cowl "parade phaeton"—for direction. The parade car featured a long upper-body crease that blended into a rear-fender kickup, a touch styled by Cliff Voss, manager of the Chrysler/Imperial Studio under Exner.

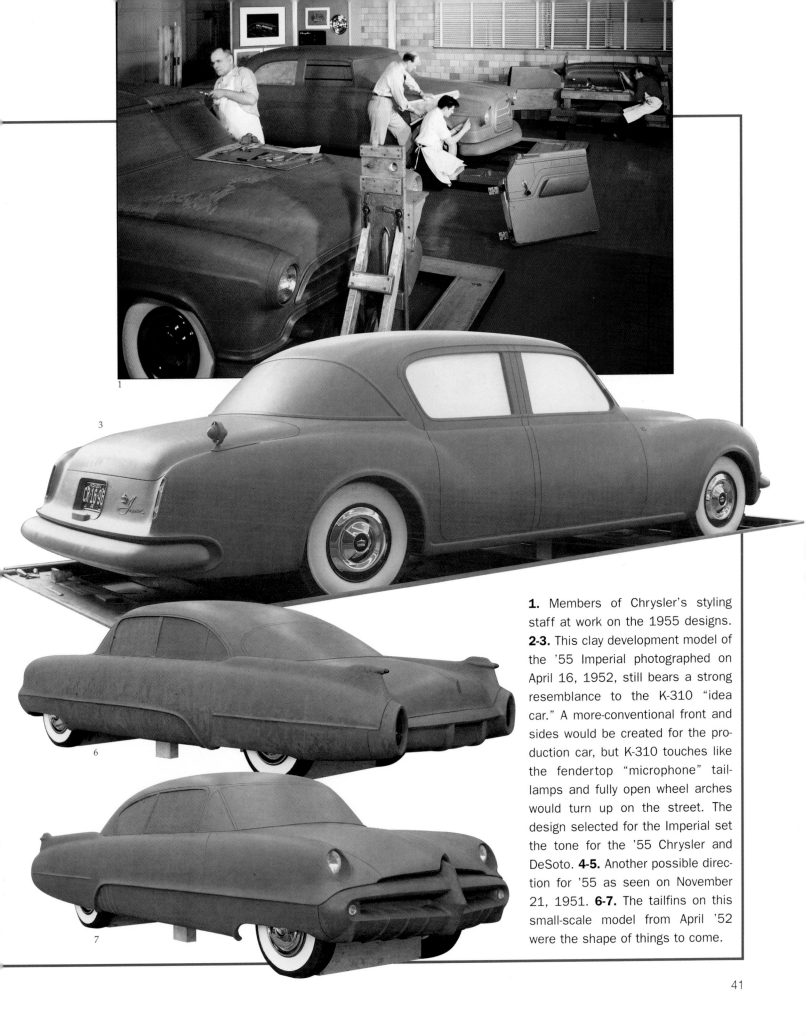

1. Members of Chrysler's styling staff at work on the 1955 designs. **2-3.** This clay development model of the '55 Imperial photographed on April 16, 1952, still bears a strong resemblance to the K-310 "idea car." A more-conventional front and sides would be created for the production car, but K-310 touches like the fendertop "microphone" taillamps and fully open wheel arches would turn up on the street. The design selected for the Imperial set the tone for the '55 Chrysler and DeSoto. **4-5.** Another possible direction for '55 as seen on November 21, 1951. **6-7.** The tailfins on this small-scale model from April '52 were the shape of things to come.

1

The first full expression of Virgil Exner's design touch was the new "Forward Look" for 1955. **1-2.** This New Yorker DeLuxe Newport hardtop shows off slab-sided styling, a broad-shouldered aspect, and a notably lower stance. Exner lieutenant Cliff Voss devised the high bodyside crease and fading rear-fender motif. **3.** The split grille on the '55 New Yorker St. Regis suggested movement. **4.** The new high-powered C-300 mixed Windsor side trim with the face of an Imperial.

3

2

4

1957 CHRYSLER

1

3

4

If General Motors gets the credit (or perhaps the blame) for introducing the tailfin to American cars, then it's Chrysler that takes the prize for making fins beautiful. All five Chrysler Corporation makes sported dramatic new trajectories from their rear-quarter sheetmetal, but perhaps none had a more graceful or "natural" treatment than the corporation's namesake brand.

Virgil Exner's fondness for Italian design, which in the mid Fifties included the wildly finned Alfa Romeo BAT cars, had an influence. So did wind tunnel tests that demonstrated some added stability from fins. Low hoods and thin, flat roof panels were other elements of the '57 look.

6

7

1-2. A clay styling model from November 11, 1954, shows the low beltine and soaring fin blades that would be central elements of the 1957 Chryslers. **3-4.** Fin motifs sprouted on corporate show cars like the 1955 FlightSweep I (3) and '57 Dart (4). **5.** By late July '56, only minor details remained to be resolved. The lower trim on this New Yorker's side ultimately would be extended into the front fender. **6-9.** This over-the-top rear proposal for the mighty 300 was fortunately rejected.

1

Chrysler president L. L. Colbert and design chief Virgil Exner hit home runs for 1957, eschewing the self-conscious futurism of some concept studies in favor of swoopy elegance of production cars that were long, low, and sleek in the extreme. **1.** The '57 New Yorker ragtop saw just 1049 examples. Rear fins rose gracefully from the fendertops; dramatically backswept wheel arches imparted a sense of speed and forward movement. **2.** The new models' graceful rooflines are clear on this New Yorker hardtop sedan. Chrysler's closed cars had a purity of design that even the convertibles lacked. **3.** The design easily accepted quad headlights for cars sold where such equipment was legal.

2

3

1

2

1. A trapezoidal grille was among the more obvious of the powerful 300-C's distinguishing features. As with other 1957 Chryslers, the 300 was long, slim, and sculptured, yet relatively restrained in its decoration. **2.** The towering tailfins ended in tall wedges of taillight. A "shadow box" in the decklid held the license plate. Design chief Virgil Exner was a great fan of Italian auto designs, particularly the wildly finned Alfa Romeo BAT 9 of 1955.

1958 CHRYSLER

The quest for visual novelty made Fifties Detroit the home of the annual facelift. For automakers that could afford it, all-new styling would come around every two or three years, with changes to grilles, taillamps, and side trim in between.

Chrysler used these tricks to touch up its '58s. Also, quad headlights, an option in '57, were made standard.

1-2. This Windsor proposal from October '56 sports a front end ultimately reserved for 1958 New Yorkers and Saratogas. The visor over the rear window never reached production. **3.** The production '58 New Yorker actually had *less* side trim than the '57 model.

1

2

3

1959 CHRYSLER

Designers often say the first version of a design is the "purest," and every subsequent facelift increasingly detracts from it. For the third go-round on the 1957 body, Chrysler stylists worked hard to create some substantial difference in the '59s.

While 300s kept a trapezoidal grille, others had a new face in which the headlights appeared to be sinking into the grille. A sharp peak rose over revised taillights, and a shallow decklid sat above a massive rear bumper.

1

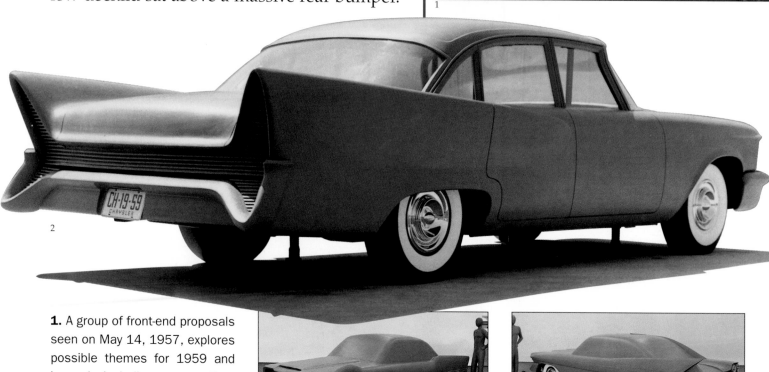
2

1. A group of front-end proposals seen on May 14, 1957, explores possible themes for 1959 and beyond—including one very Pontiac-like twin-grille look. **2.** This clay model under development a year earlier indicates that a lot of attention was being given to changing the Chrysler's rear end for 1959. The shallow decklid on the model would carry over for the production car, as would rooftop sculpting. **3-6.** A sample of advanced-design explorations for late-Fifties Chryslers as modeled in 1955 (3-5) and '57 (6).

3

4

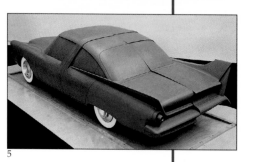
5

6

7. Following two seasons of simple brightwork applications, the '59 Windsor displayed a busier bodyside. The tall, imposing rear bumper was a departure from 1957-58. **8.** The 300-E continued with an update of its unique grille. **9.** Graceless lamp brows marred the '59 New Yorker. The grille retained a full-width look.

orporate body sharing being what it was, DeSoto began the Fifties with the same high, square-rigged look of its bigger Chrysler brother. Apart from the wheelbase distinctions, each make employed its own frontal styling and trim details.

Thick, vertical grille teeth, a DeSoto styling touch since the early Forties, remained in evidence as the new decade began. Hardtop styling arrived for 1950. A 1951 update to the '49-vintage body included more glass area and a pronounced crease that trailed from the hood into the front fenders.

1. Small-scale models from October 1948 tried out fully skirted wheels. **2-4.** A more-conventional look as seen on November 2, 1948. **5-6.** The 1951 DeSoto (5) was an evolutionary update of the '50 model (6).

Virgil Exner's first breath of fresh air upon the styling at Chrysler gave a lift to the '53 DeSoto. It shared in the companywide shift to one-piece windshields, and, like Chrysler, it gained a wraparound backlight for four-door sedans and club coupes.

DeSotos continued with updated versions of specific styling touches like the toothy grille and a hood scoop introduced on 1952's first V-8 models. The "floating" '54 grille became a favorite of car customizers.

1. This propped-up full-size rendering from August 1950 has the one-piece windshield and wrapped rear window that would appear on production cars for 1953-54. **2-3.** An earlier ⅜-scale clay model showed a GM-like six-window roof design. **4.** Actual '53s, like the FireDome convertible, featured prominent rear fenders. **5.** The grille, bumpers, and side trim were redone for 1954.

1

2

A s DeSoto shared bodies with Chrysler and the newly independent Imperial, it also made use of the parade-phaeton-inspired styling applied to its costlier siblings for 1955. Of course, different taillights, grilles, and side trim lent distinction to each make.

DeSoto used a vertical-tooth grille for the last time in 1955. The oversized "fangs" at the far ends of this ensemble served as high-riding bumper "bombs." The considerably flatter hood incorporated a scoop motif at its forward edge.

5

1-2. Side trim for 1955's high-line Fireflites combined the treatments seen on both sides of this December 1952 clay. 3-4. A Mercury-like model from early '53 had less influence. 5. Studio modelers finish interior and exterior clays. 6. Fireflite Coronados featured tri-tone paint. 7-9. Fireflites (7, 9) had rocker-panel and headlight trim that Firedomes (8) lacked.

1957-59 DeSOTO

The small fins that sprouted from the rear of Chrysler cars in 1956 rose into full bloom for 1957. Stylists working on Virgil Exner's low-waisted, high-tailed beauties strove to create brand distinction within the Forward Look concept, then had to provide visual updates for 1958 and '59.

"Tri-tower" taillights—a stack of three round lenses in each fin blade first tried in '56—replaced a toothy grille as DeSoto's signature styling touch through the remainder of the decade. A combined bumper/grille with an elongated ovoid opening appeared in 1957-58, then was modified into two smaller slots for '59.

1. The DeSoto take on the '54 Chrysler clay model seen on pages 44-45. **2.** Elements of 1957 Plymouth, Dodge, and DeSoto mix in this June '56 hardtop station wagon mock-up. **3.** An illustration from April 5, 1956, of a possible '58 touch-up. **4.** Studio modelers work on the '57s. **5-6.** A 1959 proposal with stacked headlights from May '56. **7-8.** Other ideas from July (7) and August (8) 1956.

1. Gold contrast paint, badges, and wheel covers adorned the 1957 DeSoto Adventurer. 2. Firesweep, a lower-cost line added for '57, borrowed the chassis, hood, and fenders of that year's Dodge. 3. Regardless of series or body, two-toned '57 DeSotos used the pattern seen on this Adventurer. 4-5. For '58, a fine mesh filled the revised grille; exhaust ports were crimped. 6. DeSoto details were added to the Chrysler body in '59.

4

5

6

1951-52 DODGE

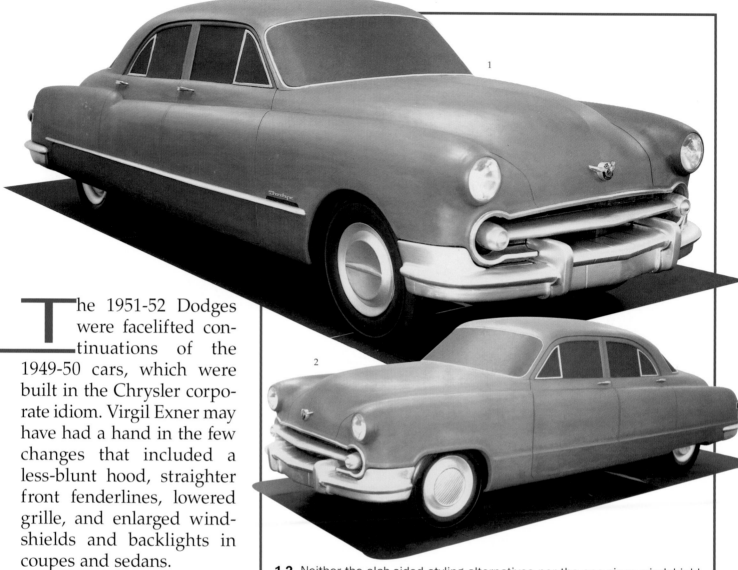

The 1951-52 Dodges were facelifted continuations of the 1949-50 cars, which were built in the Chrysler corporate idiom. Virgil Exner may have had a hand in the few changes that included a less-blunt hood, straighter front fenderlines, lowered grille, and enlarged windshields and backlights in coupes and sedans.

Trim details separated the '51s from the '52s. Wheel covers were changed, too.

1-2. Neither the slab-sided styling alternatives nor the one-piece windshield of this October 1948 clay model found their way onto early Fifties Dodges. **3-4.** The 1951 styling updates to the 1949-50 body made even the "small" Dodge, the 115-inch-wheelbase Wayfarer, appear a little longer and lower.

A good 20 years before "down-sizing" became a buzzword in Detroit, Dodge tried it on its 1953-54 cars. Wheelbase length was shortened to 119 inches for sedans, club coupes, and four-door wagons, and 114 inches for all other models.

The grille played off the look of the 1951-52 cars. A single-pane windshield and unbroken fenderline were new.

1. A February 3, 1950, clay of a coupe already has the forward-sloped C-pillar and smooth bodysides that would come in for 1953. **2-3.** Another model, this from late April '50, displays much of the final profile of the sedans. Big fender skirts wouldn't make production. **4-5.** In November '52, this finned update of the design was in the works.

Dodge was lower and sleeker for 1953. Professional testers liked the car's looks, visibility, and roominess. But improvements to bodyshells and interiors were undercut by the V-8-only "Gyro-Torque" semiautomatic transmission, which mustered painfully pokey getaways from a dead stop, and had to be clutch-and-shift manipulated between low- and high-range gears. **1-2.** The revised styling was a clear selling point, however. The flagship line was called Coronet; this is a Coronet Eight convertible with dramatic V-8 hood emblem, shapely yet understated bodyside chrome, and the new single-piece windshield. Subtle bulges at the wheel arches were a nice touch. **3-4.** A Royal convertible paced the 1954 Indianapolis 500, which opened the door for a 701-unit

3

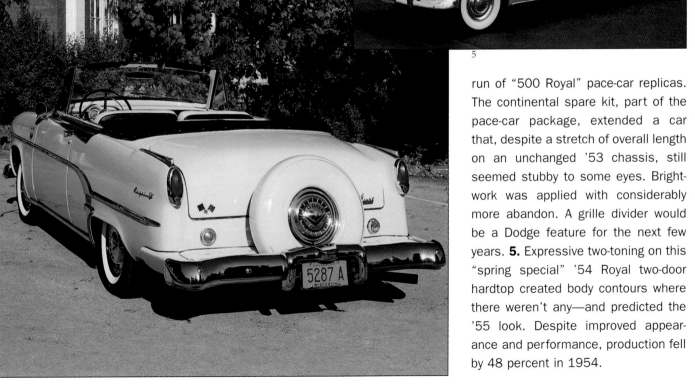

5

run of "500 Royal" pace-car replicas. The continental spare kit, part of the pace-car package, extended a car that, despite a stretch of overall length on an unchanged '53 chassis, still seemed stubby to some eyes. Brightwork was applied with considerably more abandon. A grille divider would be a Dodge feature for the next few years. **5.** Expressive two-toning on this "spring special" '54 Royal two-door hardtop created body contours where there weren't any—and predicted the '55 look. Despite improved appearance and performance, production fell by 48 percent in 1954.

4

1 9 5 6 D O D G E

Nineteen fifty-six was a facelift year for Virgil Exner's Forward Look cars, but it took a backward glance to see what was truly new about them. The softly rounded sheetmetal of the '55 cars' rear fenders had now been raised into crisp-edged integral tailfins.

The startlingly new look of the 1955 Dodge was due

in large part to the efforts of Exner protégé Maury Baldwin. The essential design stayed the same for '56, but for the fins that began rising at a low angle from a point just below the roof C-pillar. (Some wagons used tacked-on chrome fins that approximated the same shape.) Round taillights and back-up lamps filled the boomerang-shaped opening that formed under the fins.

In front, a simulated scoop was added to the chrome trim that ran over the hood.

1. A single grille bar was ultimately rejected. **2-3.** This fin/taillight concept would have made the '58 Cadillac look like a copycat. **4.** A windshield visor and heftier grille bar were proposed. **5.** The tail was nearing completion by July 1954. **6-7.** Top-line '56 Custom Royals (6) had body-color headlamp surrounds that Royals (7) did not.

6

1

2

3

4

Dodge called its iteration of Chrysler's 1957 styling revolution "Swept-Wing." Unlike the other Mopar brands, Dodge fins didn't reach fully to the end of the car. This, and chrome that ran from the base of the fins to their raised peaks, made them appear to be tacked on.

Hoods sat flush with the fendertops. Sedan and two-door hardtop roofs were supported by slender pillars. Quad headlamps were easily adapted in 1958. A heavy '59 frontal redo reintegrated the headlights with the front sheetmetal, while in back, additional chrome adorned revised fins.

1. A clay model shows '57 Dodge fins were more a part of the body than they appeared in production. 2. A view of the wagon from page 56 showing more of its Dodge influence. 3-4. A May '56 clay proposed enlarged rear lights and a "knitted brow" grille for '59. 5-6. The concept had developed into this by July. 7-8. Side trim and taillights were still unresolved in February 1957. 9. The Regal Lancer wasn't built.

1. The formal grille crest adorning this '57 Custom Royal Lancer was long and lean, like nearly every other design aspect of Dodge's all-new line. Hardly taller than an adolescent boy, the new Dodges had well-integrated headlamp/parking-lamp ensembles, a single-bar grille, gracefully sloped rooflines, and strikingly thin roof pillars. **2.** If there was a problem, it was the "afterthought" appearance of the Dodge fins—an unfortunate illusion caused by fin length, chrome accents, and color patterns. This is a '57 Coronet Lancer. **3.** A Coronet shows off the reworked grille and quad headlights for '58. **4.** The Regal Lancer, offered only in 1958, featured complex two-toning. **5-6.** For '59s like these Custom Royal Lancer convertibles, headlamps were returned to the front sheetmetal, chrome wedges capped reshaped fins, and angle-cut bezels held rear lights.

3

4

5

6

1

2

3

After gaining separate-make status for 1955, Imperial went a step further in '57. It got its own bodyshells, which let Virgil Exner create an enhanced version of the second generation of the Forward Look.

Late-Fifties Imperials mixed "classic" touches like biplane bumpers (on the '57s) and an optional faux spare-tire cover with new ideas like curved side-window glass.

6

7

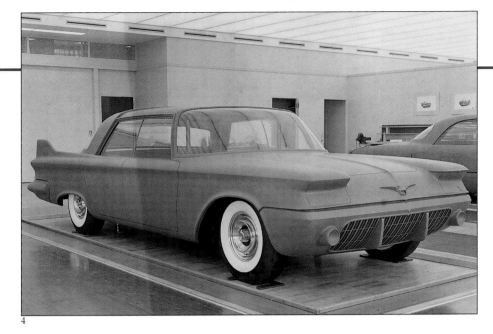

4

5

1. Good progress toward the eventual shape of the 1957 Imperial was being made by November 1954, when this full-size clay model was photographed. The prominent, straight-edged headlamp hoods were an homage to the arcing front fenders of classic-era cars like the Cord L-29. 2-3. Explorations for possible designs for 1959 and beyond included this clay from July 27, 1956. Its fins rise from midbody to tall, rudderlike blades somewhat like those seen on the '57 Chrysler 300 mock-up on pages 44 and 45. 4-5. The front of this model from October '56 shows much kinship with the 1958 D'Elegance II show car. Toned-down versions of various elements seen here turned up on the 1960 Imperial. 6-8. The general look of the 1957 Imperial stayed put for three years, but a clay from May 3, 1956, shows the '59 facelift could have been more drastic.

8

Model year 1957 kicked off Imperial's dead-on run at the luxury segment dominated by Cadillac. **1.** Design chief Virgil Exner's philosophy of "arrested motion" is realized in the swoopy '57 Imperial Crown Southampton four-door hardtop. The broad, sloped deck—seen here with optional dummy spare-tire cover—was striking, but cut into storage space. Standard decklids were bisected by a smart vertical crease. The canopy roof invited two-toning. **2.** The faux spare-tire cover was just one of Exner's purposeful nods to the past. The heavy, chrome-accented headlamp brows at the front of this Southampton two-door hardtop recalled the peak of the Cord L-29's front fenders. **3-4.** For '58, Imperial side trim remained restrained; Exner's aerodynamic "wedge" profile was thought not to need excessive adornment. The Imperial sedan (3) gave up nothing in looks to the Crown hardtop coupe (4). Despite the drama of the gun-sight taillamps, the lenses were deliberately made subordinate to the fins. **5.** An elegant, single-loop rear bumper, as on this LeBaron Southampton, replaced the previous twin-element unit in 1959. **6.** This two-door Crown shows the heavier side trim added in '59. The lowered headlamps looked lost amidst the toothy, over-emphatic chrome of the revised grille.

4

6

Like Dodge, Plymouth went for a new look for 1953 that did away with the notion of separate rear fenders. Dimensions were tidier, too, with a wheelbase that was 4.5 inches shorter than that of the biggest 1949-52 Plymouths. (Gone, too, was the short-chassis series with its three-seat coupe and fastback sedan.)

Henry King's Plymouth stylists penned coupe and sedan roofs that differed from those used on the otherwise similar Dodges.

1-2. A ⅜-scale clay model from April 27, 1950, bears the slab-sided body, single-pane windshield, and bisected trapezoidal grille opening of the '53 Plymouths. Greenhouse details were still in flux, but the "through" fenderline and vertical taillight placement were already evident. **3-4.** Another model from earlier in the same month showed bold side sculpting, a "Darrin-dip" fenderline, an ellpitical grille cavity, and wraparound taillights that would not survive. **5-6.** Grille and roofline ideas took shape on a full-size clay that was in the works on September 8, 1950. **7-8.** Like its Big Three rivals, Chrysler Corporation had considered small-car projects since the mid Thirties, but wouldn't introduce one until 1960. This proposed Plymouth Cadet, as seen in clay on September, 18, 1951, could have been ready for 1953 or '54.

5

6

7

8

1

2

3

4

Plymouth promoted the "truly balanced ride" of its '53s, which meant that the new straightline *styling* was fresh but unthreatening. **1.** Wheelbase was reduced by 4.5 inches, to a uniform 114, as on this Cranbrook Belvedere two-door hardtop. Chrome trim on the character line that extended from the grille emphasized the hooded front-wheel arches. **2.** A matching extrusion at the rear, as seen on this Cranbrook convertible, kept the rear-quarter panels from appearing too tall. **3.** Visibility improved with the adoption of a one-piece windshield. **4.** The C-pillar and backlight designs of this Cranbrook club coupe weren't shared with any other Chrysler products.

Plymouth shook off its lumpy, frumpy image in a big way for 1955. It helped to add about a foot in length, a stretch that gained even more visual impact from forward-leaning front fenders and rear quarters that reached back over the vertical taillights. Studio stylist Charles "Bud" Gitschlag was chiefly responsible for the look.

The corporate embrace of fins showed up on the '56s. The grille was redone, too.

1. A clay model from April 1953 has a grille nearly identical to the accepted '55 design, but the rest of the body looks like it was borrowed from a 1954 Dodge. **2.** This hardtop mock-up seen on March 24, 1952, also suggests an evolutionary change was originally in the works. **3.** Twin grille pods were eyed in 1954 for the '56 facelift.

4

5

6

Play-it-safe Plymouth design for 1954 opened the door for Buick and Oldsmobile to surpass it in sales, but Chrysler's volume make got it right for '55. **4.** This Belvedere sedan shows the new hooded headlights and the forward lean of the body. **5.** A Belvedere hardtop displays its wrapped windshield. Side trim and color patterns produced some unorthodox shapes. **6.** A ledge under the trunklid conveyed continuity from 1953 and '54.

1

2

Sharp, dramatically canted "Flight Sweep" fins were the centers of attention on the '56 Plymouths. Indeed, because money for retooling was tight, design chief Virgil Exner focused on revisions to the rear-quarter panels. **1.** Belvedere side trim was modified and lowered, giving a busy, scrunched look. Side skirts were available, but made two-tone Plymouths appear bottom-heavy. The four-door hardtop body was new to Plymouth. **2.** Bodyside trim was far cleaner on the new high-performance Fury, and flowed congenially with the basic lines of the car. Up front, the center of the grille was given a mesh-fronted box, with a gold "V" for V-8 models. **3.** The fins looked prodigious framing the two-piece tailgate of the Sport Suburban wagon. Vertical chrome strakes at the rear hinted at the fabulous Chevy Nomad.

3

When advertising for the '57 Plymouth proclaimed, "Suddenly, it's 1960," one look proved the statement wasn't at all far-fetched. A "shark-fin" tail created unprecedented (for Plymouth) drama at the rear. A low, straight beltline and thin roof panels transformed Chrysler's humble budget make into a tailored, very suave car-about-town. When designers from General Motors's formidable styling section got their first look at these Plymouths in late summer 1956, they ran back to totally rethink the '59 models on which they were working.

Other details accentuated existing themes. The forward-leaning fender edges of 1955-56 adopted an even-more rakish angle. The fins were filled with taller versions of recent years' triangular taillights.

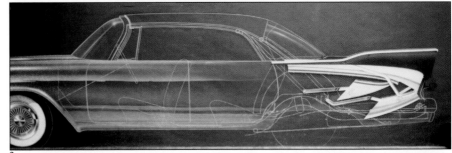

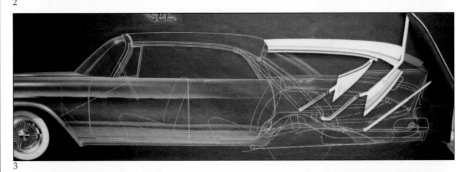

1. This rendering with a possible side-trim workup for the Belvedere clearly shows the sleek fins and thin roof section that made the '57 Plymouth a breakthrough design. **2-5.** Styling departments didn't just dream up fresh sheetmetal; sometimes they came up with proposals for new types of vehicles, like this never-built Phaeton four-door retractable convertible. **6.** The Plainsman was an "idea car" for the 1956 show season that held a lot of influence for Chrysler station wagon designers. **7-8.** The Cabana, seen as a mock-up on September 27, 1955, was Plymouth designers' take on the Plainsman for a possible hardtop station wagon. **9.** Another suggested approach to bodyside brightwork for the top-line Belvedere series.

Plymouth reinvented itself for 1957 with its "Suddenly, it's 1960" look. Chrysler president L. L. "Tex" Colbert was determined that Plymouth regain the number-three spot in industry sales. **1.** Side trim on the '57 Fury two-door hardtop had the basic shape seen on the studio drawing on page 82, but added a smart back-to-front rise very much in keeping with the wildly forward-thrusting nose. **2-3.** Belvedere two- and four-door hardtops with towering, well-integrated fins, elegantly thin roof pillars—and some horizontal-vertical conflict between the grille and the under-bumper valance designs. Headlights were not true quads, as the inboard lenses were actually parking lights. **4.** Bottom-heavy trim and color treatment was apparent on some Savoy models. The sidespear and ivory-color body tone sit low enough to make the car appear as if it's riding on its rear frame. **5.** Although not as eye-catching as two-tones, monochrome '57s, such as this Belvedere convertible, had a kind of purity, even if the tailfins were coming close to Lincoln territory. The two-toning on this car was on the upholstery. Note the oblong horn ring, a clear touch of Exner.

1958 PLYMOUTH

A year of dramatic styling in 1957 was followed by a stand-pat year that relied on detail changes to create a degree of novelty. The biggest change of note was a switch to quad headlights—now legal in all 48 states—though even they fit easily into fenders that had accommodated dual headlights with large inboard parking-light lenses for '57.

The previous year's vertical cooling slots under the front bumper were replaced by a section of horizontal bars that looked like a continuation of the full-width grille. Red taillight lenses supplanted the round back-up lights of '57, and, when paired with a chrome spear that filled the space of the former taillamps, imparted a "lollipop" look. New Fury and Belvedere side trim emphasized the rise of the fins.

1

2

3

1-2. In late March '56, Plymouth stylists were considering edging the wheel openings in chrome and making some radical taillight changes for 1958. The hardtop's switch to the convertible's compound-curve windshield would have to wait one more year, however. 3. A 1958-style update of the Cabana station wagon theme as seen on October 11, 1956. 4. By early August '56, major details of the 1958 facelift were worked out. This styling model shows the new wheel covers, taillights, and rear bumper (with integral centered back-up light) that would be approved. 5. Side trim was still not set in stone even as late as November '56. 6. Months earlier, this solid bumper was eyed.

1

2

3

4

Minor design tweaks marked the 1958 Plymouths. Real change was expensive and unnecessary, for Plymouth took back its number-three industry spot for '57 when it outsold Buick by 300,000 units. Plymouth assemblies rocketed to more than 729,000 for '57, a 44 percent increase. **1.** New "jet-fin" ornaments appeared on the front fendertops of '58 Furys, Belvederes, and Savoys; this is a Belvedere hardtop coupe. **2.** Vertical air intakes under the bumper were dropped, bringing a more-unified front end. Quad headlights were now universally legal, and Plymouth showed them proudly, as on this Belvedere four-door hardtop. **3-4.** A Savoy hardtop coupe and Savoy four-door sedan, with new circular taillights and "PLYMOUTH" decklid. The sedan has the most-modest available side treatment.

The styling kinship of the last Plymouth of the Fifties to its 1957-58 forebears was obvious, but the '59 was still substantially changed. As with the year's other Chrysler Corporation makes, the alterations ran from nose to tail.

A front bumper with a slight dip in the center replaced the bridge-style unit of recent years. Fender edges still had their dramatic forward thrust, but instead of dropping to the bumpers, they stopped halfway down, then ran back over the front-wheel openings. Once-flat fendertops now appeared to trace the contour over each of the four headlights. The grille adopted a tighter eggcrate pattern and projected a greater sense of depth than in the past.

Modified fins took on a longer arc, losing some of their "shark-fin" nature. Their trailing edges now leaned forward and were edged in chrome. Taillights newly stood free in elliptical bezels.

1-2. Long, straight fins in the Chrysler/DeSoto mold were considered on this clay model from late January '56. **3-4.** Fin and fender treatments akin to the final production styles began to emerge by March 3. **5-6.** Other refinements were obvious on wagon and sedan models photographed just a few weeks later. **7.** The idea of using a badge centered in the grille was being tested when this full-scale clay was shown on July 26, 1956. The bumper is quite close to the actual production piece. **8-9.** The same model displays alternate taillight, side-trim, and bumper-guard suggestions. **10-11.** As of October 29, the grille was being bisected by a badge, a touch that would be adopted. Oblong taillights had won favor, but would be enlarged.

1

1. This Sport Fury reveals the forward-swept fins, oblong taillights (the lenses were no longer in the fins), and Imperial-like decklid that were new for '59. Furys and Sport Furys were nearly ringed in brightwork. The circular, fin-mounted medallions were exclusive to Sport Furys. **2.** A Custom Suburban wagon, with its new and exclusive rear-quarter panel; other Chrysler makes' wagons made do with carryover sheet-metal. **3.** A Sport Fury two-door hard-top stands very low (note the female model), and has contoured headlamp brows, a hunkier grille, and the longer-arc fins common to all '59 Plymouths.

2

FORD MOTOR COMPANY

Of all the American automakers, Ford sailed most easily through the Fifties (stylistically, that is), especially the company's namesake brand. The slab-sided Ford of 1949—"the car that saved an empire"—continued with modest changes through 1951. The 1952-54 Fords replaced boxiness with a taut, eager look that hinted at the V-8 often tucked underhood. With them came the round taillights that would, with one exception, adorn every Ford for the rest of the decade.

Though some criticized the 1955-56 Fords as not being sufficiently changed, they were the best Fords of the decade. The Ford Fairlane Crown Victoria Skyliner (a name that sounds like a christening of British royalty) with its "checkmark" bodyside molding, pastel two-toning, "eyebrow" headlamp bezels, and broad chrome tiara arcing over the roof offered a sharp contrast to the Customline two-door sedan and its simple front-to-back body molding. In '56, Ford adapted the lower Crown Vic windshield and roof (sans arch) for its regular two-door Victoria, giving the '56 Ford hardtops an aggressive, hot-rod look that appeared chopped because it was.

Ford fielded another attractive car with the 1957 Fairlane/Fairlane 500. Bodyside trim on 500s merged gracefully with the cars' modest canted fins. (The shorter-wheelbase Custom/Custom 300s were not as successful.) The design was clumsily facelifted for 1958, the round taillights being abandoned and the Fairlane 500's sides disfigured by an awkward swath of gold anodized aluminum trim—one reason the November 1957 issue of *Time* magazine dubbed Ford styling vice president George Walker "The Cellini of Chrome."

Round taillights triumphantly returned in 1959 on a conservatively styled car that enabled Ford to outsell the radical batwing Chevy. The midyear Galaxie, with its wide C-pillar roof lifted directly from the Thunderbird, garnered even more sales.

Mercury's path was more problematic. The slinky 1949-51 "Merc"—starting point for countless customizers and immortalized by James Dean in *Rebel Without a Cause*—was one of Bob Gregorie's favorite designs. It has transcended time to become the very soul of Mercury.

The all-new 1952-54 Mercurys, while quite attractive, looked more Ford-like, perhaps appropriate since they once again shared bodies. Aside from the Gregorie Merc, the best-looking Mercury of the decade was undoubtedly the straightlined '55, especially the midyear "chopped top" Montclair sedan.

Seeking to make Mercury more distinctive, the 1957-58 Turnpike Cruiser, with its heavy body sculpturing, retractable backlight, and other fancy geegaws, became instead an embarrassment to the Ford family. Much toned down in 1959, Mercury would have one more year to enjoy its own bodyshell before returning to glorified Ford status in 1961.

Lincoln, like Mercury, began the decade with a bulbous Gregorie design, then adopted a fleeter-appearing look for 1952-55. While excellent cars in their own right (witness the Mexican road race victories), these Lincolns were not true Cadillac competitors. Then, suddenly, unexpectedly, the 1956 Lincoln appeared. Designed in tandem with the Futura show car, the '56 Lincoln was a truly lovely car whose tasteful beauty lasted a mere year before being compromised by tacked-on tailfins.

With the planners suddenly seized by the desire to out-Cadillac Cadillac, another all-new Lincoln appeared in 1958. These mammoth cars were the largest unitized-body cars ever attempted. While their enormous flanks were commendably chrome-free, their gargantuan bulk did not find favor, and Lincoln remained adrift.

And what to say about the Edsel? Though the very name has become a synonym for failure, Ford management got what it asked for. Chief designer Roy Brown and his stylists were given the thorny task of creating a truly distinctive look—and they succeeded! What is perhaps not appreciated is that the Ford- and Mercury-based '58 Edsels were actually very different from each other. Roofs, fenders, doors, and quarter panels were all different. Watered down in 1959 and '60, Edsel production did not survive the decade. A victim of bad styling? Perhaps. Market trends were also against the car at the time of its introduction.

By contrast, the four-passenger Thunderbird that bowed in 1958 was the right car at the right time. Though widely admired, the handsome two-passenger T-Birds of 1955-57 were not big sellers. By adding a back seat, Ford created the first of the so-called "personal luxury" cars, much to the consternation of General Motors's Harley Earl, whose Motorama show cars had presaged the concept. With its sculpted flanks and signature "blind-quarter" roofline, the Thunderbird was transformed into a new kind of luxury car whose glamour was expertly mined to sell more-pedestrian Ford sedans.

Compare the successful Thunderbird with the eagerly awaited Continental Mark II. Introduced for 1956 with high hopes and a $10,000 price tag, the Mark II was too imitative of the past to be a successful design. It tried too hard to be a Forties Continental, even to the point of placing the signature "continental" spare tire right in the way of retrieving anything in the trunk.

1958 EDSEL

Ford Motor Company's desire to broaden its reach in the medium-price field resulted in one of the most famous flops in industry history: the Edsel. Introduced to the public in September 1957, production lasted only until November 1959. Ford lost an estimated $250 million on the program.

Design work for the "E" car—as the Edsel was known at Ford before its name had been selected—began as early as 1954. The studio was headed by Roy Brown, Jr., a native of Canada who began his styling career at General Motors in the Thirties, but who was plucked from the Lincoln Studio for the Edsel job.

The '58 Edsels came in four trim levels; two shared bodies with costlier Mercurys and two were based on cheaper Fords. All featured the controversial "horse-collar" grille that was Edsel's dominant style feature.

1

2

3

4

1-3. A vertical grille element was considered for the Edsel from the start. These drawings are by Roy Brown's assistant, Robin Jones, who had experimented with the idea earlier while at Packard. 4. A gullwing deck theme also arose early. 5. Allowances were made for an anticipated shift to quad headlamps by 1958. 6-7. The vertical center bar was opened up at the urging of Ford CEO Ernest Breech. Early versions of the design were called Ventura. 8-9. The Ford-based "E" car in early summer '55. 10. The Mercury-based design, July 1955. 11. The rear and sides neared final form in August.

1

2

3

4

Edsel's "horse-collar" grille fulfilled the Fifties design protocol that a car be instantly recognizable, but also made the new make appear as if it wanted to fall onto its too-heavy face. **1.** The Ford-based Pacer ragtop for 1958 was arguably the best-looking model of the inaugural line, with a graceful, second-color side cove aft, and a subdued sidespear. **2.** The boomerang taillight lenses of the Bermuda "Edselized" a station wagon body that had to be shared with Ford for economy's sake. **3.** A layered side-cove design competed with the grille of the Mercury-based '58 Citation, and was, frankly, overwrought. **4.** Split front bumpers, as seen on this Citation hardtop, parted to make way for the aggressive grille. **5.** The attractively sculpted deck, seen here on the Merc-derived Corsair, was hurt by an unreasonably massive expanse beneath narrow taillamps.

5

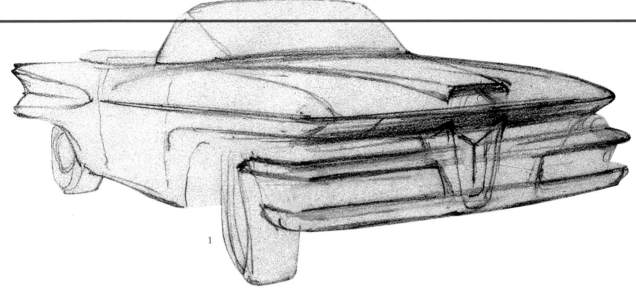

1

With the Edsel off to a slow start for its debut season—which turned out to be a sales-robbing recession year—enthusiasm for the car at Ford was cooling rapidly. The '59 lineup was trimmed substantially to two series related to the Ford Fairlane.

Not only did designers have to abandon the Mercury-like cars, but they were directed to tone down the controversial center grille. The 1959 version of the "horse collar" was shorter and flatter than its predecessor. Meanwhile, headlamps were lowered into the grille.

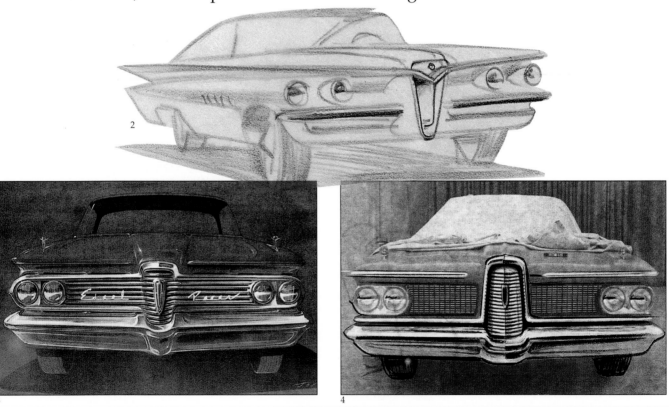

2

3

4

1-2. A pair of Robin Jones's early sketches for the 1959 Edsel showed a "Y" element added to the vertical grille. The hardtop sketch also includes the kind of lowered headlight placement many American cars would adopt for '59. **3.** In an effort to diminish the prominence of the center grille, Jones drew this design, but tooling plans were too far along to accommodate it. **4.** A vertical grille that widened toward the bottom and headlights set in heavy chrome bezels were other ideas that were ultimately rejected for for the '59 Edsel program. **5-6.** When the two high-line series that shared bodies with Mercury were canceled, these possible trim variations went for naught. **7.** Edsel designers never did quite give up on the vertical center-blade idea, as seen on this mock-up.

1

2

3

4

5

Mercury bodies were no longer used by Edsel for 1959, which was probably to the good, but the Ford sourcing became even more obvious this year. **1-2.** The Corsair convertible showed the design studio's attempt to diminish the horse collar by narrowing the surround and bringing it nearly flush with the rest of the grillework. At the rear, the sculpting of the deck was flattened. Revised taillamps were sited lower, but looked a bit droopy. A full-length sidespear with delta insert identified the new top-line series. **3.** A Ranger two-door sedan displays new chrome headlamp brows and tacked-on fendertop ornamentation. The sidespear delta looked better in body color. The side cove had been deleted. **4-5.** The lowering of headlamps into the grille, as on this Ranger sedan, was a new Detroit trend. The roof was pure Ford Fairlane.

1

Having begun the Fifties with facelifted versions of its highly successful 1949 model, Ford needed to come up with a sparkling, modern encore for 1952. The backdrop for this process was the politically charged atmosphere that pitted outside consultant George Walker's designers against Ford Motor Company's in-house stylists.

The resulting car expanded on and updated themes from the 1949 to 1951 period. It more bore the stamp of Walker protégé Joe Oros than it did of the Ford Studio stylists under the direction of Frank Bianchi.

2

1. This small-scale clay model from 1949 shows a few touches that would be picked up for the 1952 Fords, such as a one-piece windshield and a flared stamping in the rear bodysides. The "spinner" grille, a prominent feature of the '49 Ford, was expected to be carried on. **2.** Styling studio staff members complete a full-size side-elevation rendering of the '52 four-door sedan body. **3-4.** Clays photographed in June 1950 show prospective grille variations. The station wagon body was worked up by the Body Development Studio headed by Gordon Buehrig. **5.** A George Barbaz rendering of a panel van with elements of the new car design.

1

2

3

4

5

1. The spinner grille motif of 1949-51 was retained for '52, as seen on this Victoria hardtop. Skirts and a dealer-installed chrome strip above the side sculpture are add-ons. **2.** This 1952 Sunliner's new round taillamps were destined to become a Ford styling trademark. **3-4.** For '53, "Vicky" hard-tops got a new one-piece backlight. The grille and side trim were revised. **5.** The Skyliner, a newcomer for 1954, featured a novel Plexiglas roof panel.

1955-56 FORD

Ford came into 1955 with something sort of new and something else completely new. The former was the line of Ford family cars, which was actually a thorough reskinning of the 1952-54 design. The latter was the Thunderbird, Ford's two-seat answer to the Chevrolet Corvette.

Franklin Hershey started the ball rolling—secretly— on the Thunderbird not long after he became head of the Ford design studio in 1952. By the time corporate honchos decided the following year that they wanted a car to rival the Corvette, the team Hershey had assembled already was well on the way to having a design.

1-2. Hooded headlights, front-fender sculpting, and larger "Jet-Tube" taillamps were new for the '55 Fords. Grille texture, trim details, and a switch to vertical A-pillars had yet to be resolved on these mock-ups. **3.** Bill Boyer, recruited away from General Motors, sketched this racing-inspired Thunderbird in 1953. Franklin Hershey assigned Boyer, John Samsen, and Allan Kornmiller to the Body Development Studio supervised by Damon Woods to begin work on a two-seat sports car that became the T-Bird.

4

5

4. For great looks, rakish, smartly chromed '55 Crown Victorias were hard to beat. The sun was hard to beat, too, even with the tinted "bubbletop" ahead of the distinctive "basket-handle" B-pillar. **5.** Ford's broad station wagon family continued to use a two-piece tailgate. This is the Country Sedan with seats for six. **6.** Two-tone paint was typical on '55 Fairlane Sunliners. The mesh grille and aggressively browed headlights were new for the year.

6

1

2

3

1-3. Ford roared out of the gate with the all-new 1955 Thunderbird, which carried design cues taken from the rest of the Ford line. The fender louvers were just decoration, but the hood scoop was functional. Note the spinner-style bumper guards, mesh grille, browed headlights, and rallye-flag hood emblem. Wire wheel covers were a factory option. **4-5.** The famous "portholes" in the removable hardtop arrived for '56 to aid visibility. An external spare tire freed up trunk space.

4

5

1

Many enthusiasts deem the 1957 Ford to be the most attractive postwar Ford. The wonder is that it turned out as well as it did considering that it represented a mix of ideas from George Walker's consultants and Ford's staff designers.

The in-house group, led by Franklin Hershey and, later, Bob Maguire, essentially produced the 116-inch-wheelbase Custom/Custom 300. Walker's man in the Ford Studio, Joe Oros, proposed a more expressive look, and it wound up as the 118-inch-wheelbase Fairlane/Fairlane 500. (The shared low-hood front design was an Oros concept.) Ford made its first extensive use of body sculpturing with the '57s.

3

6

9

1. A colorized adaptation of designer Pierre Crease's March 16, 1955, rendering of the '57 Ford. **2.** Competing front-design ideas are tested on a two-sided clay model. **3-5.** A variety of changing ideas about fin styles, taillight size and shape, bumper designs, and roof styles are displayed in this series. One clay even sports a side exhaust outlet (4). The small blade fins were adopted for the Custom/Custom 300 sedans and all station wagons. **6-8.** Fairlanes and Fairlane 500s featured fins that sprang from midbody. The hardtop-style two-door wagon (6) was never built. Neither were ornate sedan roofs (7). **9-10.** Because it tipped off '57 Ford styling, the Mystere was kept off the show circuit until late 1955.

Ford's slab-sided philosophy receded for 1957, and its cars appeared lower and longer. **1-2.** The "dogleg" windshield frame, "checkmark" side trim, and angled headlamp caps of this Fairlane 500 Sunliner combined to impart a sense of motion. **3.** The finlets were a little more subdued on the Country Sedan station wagon, the core of Ford's strength in the wagon market.

4. The Skyliner's rear quarter panels were extended, the deck and beltline raised, and the back seat situated on a virtual vertical to accommodate the car's retractable hardtop, a marvel of wiring, motors, relays, and circuit breakers. **5.** The '57 Custom 300 two-door sedan was businesslike, but hardly demure. Note the rear-fender bulge and the deeply sculpted wheel arches.

1

2

3

The production life of the sporty two-seat car that Frank Hershey and his covert band began hatching in 1952 proved to be brief—just three model years. Still, in that short time, the name Thunderbird became synonymous with the idea of lively luxury in a motor car.

While the T-Bird's basic concept remained the same as in 1955-56, the '57 version was extensively face-lifted. In front, the blade bumper and its projectile-like guards were replaced by a bumper that bowed in the center to expose the grille. Raised end sections in the bumper incorporated the parking lights.

Out back, the deck was lengthened by five inches to create more trunk space for the spare tire. Thin, canted fins similar to those on the Ford Fairlanes topped the fenders, and a raised-center bumper was adopted.

4

5

6

7

8

9

10

1-4. Sketches by William Boyer and Damon Woods from July 1955 demonstrate the attention devoted to coming up with a totally new look for the rear of the 1957 Thunderbird. Though round taillights were by then something of a Ford brand signature, T-Bird stylists apparently didn't feel bound to them. **5-7.** Thick, thin, and even horizontal fins were drawn up in the quest for ideas for the '57. **8-9.** A two-sided clay model gave designers the chance to weigh alternate ideas as they were refined. The right half shows progress toward the eventually accepted design while the left half gives vent to some very fanciful taillight and bumper treatments. **10-11.** As details such as door handles, the grille, and front bumper were rounding into shape, the notion of a front-fender cove persisted for some time. **12.** By early 1956, only trim details remained to be settled.

11

12

1

2

1-3. Model year 1957 brought the last of the first-generation T-Birds. The simple, low-blade front bumper of 1956 was replaced with a taller piece that encompassed the parking lights and had a grille-framing dip in the middle. Out back, the bumper picked up a "handlebar" look, with horizontal exhaust ports at each end. The deck was longer now (and still enclosed the spare), and the modest fins were newly bladelike. These and other changes amounted to a heavy facelift, yet the general look of the 1955 and '56 models was wisely retained. **4.** Painted rims, hubcaps, and unskirted rear wheels lend a purposeful sports-racer look to this Thunderbird equipped with the supercharged 312-cid V-8 offered only in '57.

1958 FORD

Ford Motor Company's two-pronged styling apparatus in which consultant George Walker's designers competed against the company stylists ended in 1955. Walker gained full control of the process that May when he was made a Ford vice president.

Walker's lieutenants, Joe Oros and Elwood Engel, were also hired by Ford. In early 1956, Oros was named head of the Ford Studio, where work was under way on the 1958 models. Company chiefs wanted the '58 to reflect the look of the all-new Thunderbird, which led to an ungainly facelift of the pretty '57 Ford.

6

7

8

9

10

1-2. These two mock-ups, with deviations from the grille and side-trim patterns selected for 1957 production, were reviewed alongside models that more clearly had the eventual '58 Ford look to them. **3.** A major goal for the 1958 facelift would be fitting quad headlamps to the '57-style body. **4.** Had this model's flat-top four-door hardtop roof been adopted, it would have beaten GM to the punch by a year. **5.** This heavily sculpted model with a predictive compound-curve windshield was badged Parklane. **6-8.** Directed to play off the looks of the new-generation Thunderbird, Ford Studio chief Joe Oros did what he could. A hood scoop and the honeycomb grille surface were among the borrowed T-Bird cues. **9-10.** Oblong taillight housings were another motif cribbed from the 'Bird.

One of Joe Oros's earliest decisions as head of the Ford Division styling studio was to put Bill Boyer in charge of the Thunderbird program. Boyer, who had been involved with T-Bird design from the start, took over at a critical time.

Though it was widely admired and had established a name for itself, the two-seat Thunderbird had limited sales appeal. To keep the model alive, Ford executives including division general manager Robert McNamara considered turning it into a four-place "personal-luxury" car and adding a two-door hardtop version.

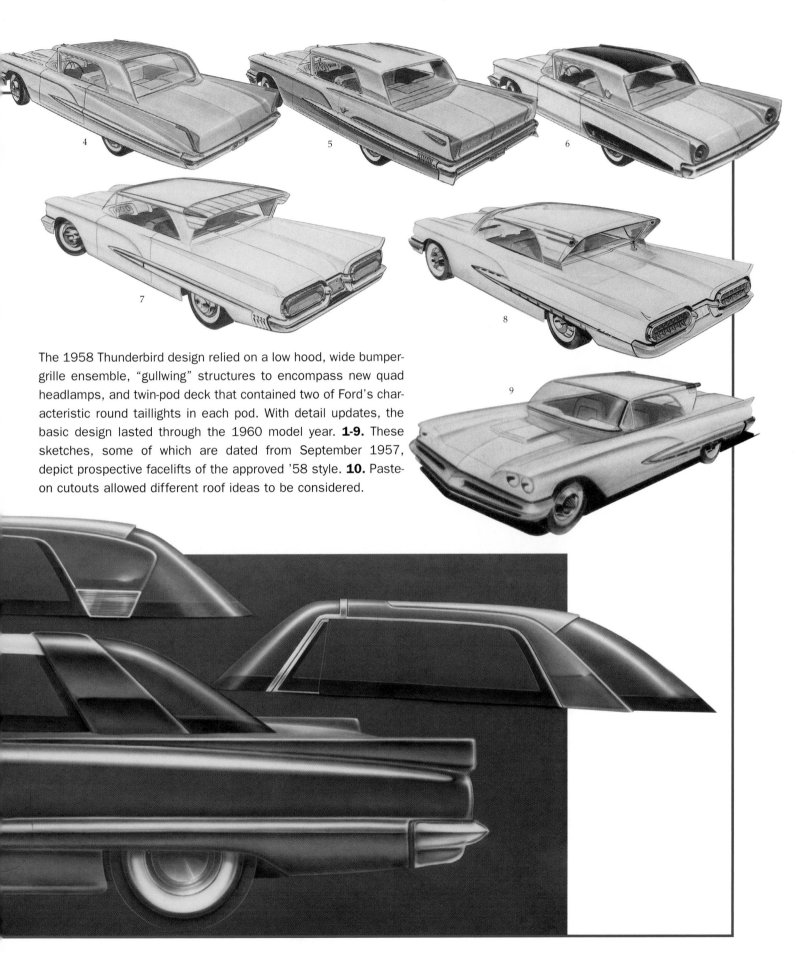

The 1958 Thunderbird design relied on a low hood, wide bumper-grille ensemble, "gullwing" structures to encompass new quad headlamps, and twin-pod deck that contained two of Ford's characteristic round taillights in each pod. With detail updates, the basic design lasted through the 1960 model year. **1-9.** These sketches, some of which are dated from September 1957, depict prospective facelifts of the approved '58 style. **10.** Paste-on cutouts allowed different roof ideas to be considered.

1

2

Bill Boyer's all-new Thunderbird hugged the ground (overall height was just 52.5 inches), yet provided sufficient room for four—attributes that could not have been realized with traditional body-on-frame construction. The unit construction that was mandated became financially possible because it had already been approved for the '58 Lincoln and Continental Mark III. All three cars came out of a new factory at Wixom, Michigan. "Squarebird" bodies, though, were built by Budd, which had built the bodies of the first-generation 'Bird. **1-2.** Gullwing headlamps suggested the car's bodyside character line. The door "bombs" that stretched forward from the rear bumper appeared on many early concept renderings. A split, deeply dipped front bumper accentuated the scoop grille, and was mimicked on the standard '58 Fords. Although most commonly skirted, the rear-wheel arches looked dramatic unadorned. **3.** The new hardtop's blind-quarter roof would be widely copied in Detroit.

3

1959 FORD

Ford went to a single chassis for model year 1959, shifting all its Customs and station wagons to the Fairlanes' longer 118-inch wheelbase. This move was accompanied by a thorough restyling that, while conservative, still netted a design award at that year's Brussels World's Fair.

While rivals were going to flat hoods and headlamps lowered into the grilles, Joe Oros directed a design that clung to a raised hood and headlights above the grille. A touch of Thunderbird style—namely the hardtop roof—topped Ford's new Galaxie-series cars.

2

3

7

6

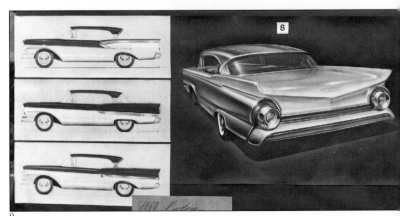

9

1. For '59, Ford adopted a vastly toned-down version of the compound-curve windshield explored on this early station wagon clay. **2-3.** A few hints of the Mystere show car flavor this sedan concept with a reverse-slant backlight. **4.** A return to round taillights was envisioned after a year off from them in '58. Inboard back-up lights wouldn't make it into production. **5.** Further refinement of the design seen in pictures 2 and 3. **6.** This group shows some of the prospective trim workups for, from top to bottom, the Custom, Fairlane, Fairlane 500, and proposed Fairlane 700. **7-8.** An arcing, thin-pillar hardtop roof would have to wait until the 1960 and '61 model years. **9.** More discarded ideas for the rear end.

127

1

2

3

4

With new, squared-off body panels and a much-changed inner structure, the '59 Fords were conservative by the standards of the day, particularly when viewed alongside the rival Chevrolet. **1-2.** These Fairlane 500 Galaxie Skyliner convertibles show the new wraparound front bumper with baby "Dagmars" and faired-in parking lights; full-width, star-motif grille; and the return of round taillamps (ads called them "Iris Eyes"). The year marked the last of the Skyliner retractable hardtops. **3.** Fins were merely suggested, as on this Galaxie four-door sedan. **4.** The Country Squire traded fake wood trim around side windows for stainless steel.

The 1950 and 1951 Lincolns were prime examples of the "upside-down bathtub" school of thought that had a number of adherents in Detroit at midcentury. The basic design had been put forth during World War II by Ford's first styling director, Eugene "Bob" Gregorie. Gregorie's related Lincoln, Lincoln Cosmopolitan, and Mercury were accepted as production designs for '49.

When Gregorie—who did not like the company's shift to a General Motors-type styling organization—left at the end of 1946, responsibility for styling Lincolns fell to William Schmidt. His studio designers undertook facelifts of the 1950-51 cars, primarily straightening the "frowning" grille of 1949.

The Continental was conspicuous by its absence. However, stylists couldn't resist conjuring up continuations of the Forties classic.

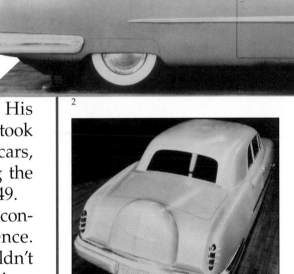

1. Lincoln design chief William Schmidt rendered this facelift proposal for the 1950 line. Its bumper/grille ensemble wasn't adopted. **2-3.** The desire to revive the Continental remained strong in the studio, as this coupe model attests. **4-5.** The 1950 Cosmopolitan (4) and base Lincoln (5) sported a grille change from '49.

Bill Schmidt, executive stylist Don DeLaRossa, and the rest of the Lincoln Studio staff had their first chance to design a car from scratch for 1952. Counter to prevailing Fifties wisdom—*especially* for luxury brands—it would be smaller than the car it was replacing.

Ford Motor Company Chief Engineer Earle MacPherson wanted a slimmer, trimmer Lincoln more competitive with the Oldsmobile 98 than with traditional rivals Cadillac and Packard. The resulting car had a lot in common, visually, with the 1952 Ford and Mercury.

1. Bill Schmidt's proposed Continental had much of the '52 Lincoln look. **2-3.** A clay model from 1949 for a possible '51 or later Lincoln. **4-5.** Production cars wore large taillights and a continuous fenderline.

I nterest in reviving the Continental would not abate, and by 1952, Ford Motor Company decided to give it a go again. (Ford went so far as to create a separate division to build the ultraluxury car.) The efforts of the division stylists were pitted against ideas submitted by four outside individuals and teams. In the end, though, it was the work of the in-house designers—headed by John Reinhart, late of Packard—that was selected for the elegant 1956 Continental Mark II hardtop coupe.

An all-new Lincoln that reverted to big luxury-car dimensions was due for '56. Bill Schmidt turned to a couple of dream cars for styling ideas.

1-2. An early model for the Continental Mark II. **3-8.** Gil Spear, head of Ford's Advanced Studio, modeled a car with a retractable hardtop. Continental Division executives heard of it, and wanted to consider the idea for their new car. They approved this prototype. **9.** Division chief William Ford (left) and stylist Bob Thomas discuss Continental design. **10-11.** The bubble-canopied Futura show car was designed in tandem with the all-new 1956 Lincoln.

2

6

7

8

10

11

1

2

Lincoln abandoned its restrained persona for 1956. **1-2.** A Premiere convertible, with new wraparound windshield, prominent rear fender ends, and hooded front wheel arches, *à la* Cadillac. Grillework was massive, but clean. **3.** The panel below the decklid copied the grille design, as seen on this Premiere two-door hardtop. **4-6.** The Continental Division, headed by William Clay Ford, aimed high and hit the mark; shapes and proportions were peerless. A dipped, "cowbelly" frame worked up by chief engineer Harley Copp allowed high seating and a low roofline. The ragtop was custom-built from a '57; the hardtop is a 1956 model.

3

4

5

6

1958-59 LINCOLN

Having returned Lincoln to true Fifties luxury-car size for 1956 and '57, the division wanted to "out-Cadillac" Cadillac for 1958. The task of how to do that visually fell to veteran Ford Motor Company designer John Najjar, who was put in charge of a newly independent Lincoln Studio in 1955.

A major influence on the general design was a motorized scale model, La Tosca. It was the brainchild of Alex Tremulis, Gil Spear's successor as head of the Advanced Studio. Diagonal quad headlamps and deep front-fender sculpting were key features of the massive 1958-59 Lincoln look.

Meanwhile, the expensive Continental Mark II lasted only until '57. There was a new Continental (Mark III in 1958 and Mark IV in '59), but it used the Lincoln body with premium appointments and a distinctive reverse-slant rear window.

2

1

3

9

8

1. One of the early proposals for the 1958 Lincoln modeled in clay in the summer of '55. 2. Clay modelers swarm over another full-sized model later in the design process. 3. John Najjar (center), head of the Lincoln Studio, discusses rear-panel designs with modelers. 4-5. Other early ideas for the car envisioned big fins inspired by the '57 Lincoln and a divided bumper/grille ensemble. 6. Though the Continental Mark II didn't last past 1957, an update of it featuring quad headlamps—which swept the industry in 1958—was eyed. 7. A fiberglass model of the '58 Continental convertible wears ultimately discarded side trim. 8-10. A two-sided model shows trim and detail alternatives for the Continental.

1

2

Continental was marketed as a separate line for 1958, but, as a money-saving measure, the Mark III and its immediate successors were based on the new unit-construction Lincoln body. The exclusive Mark II had sold very poorly, so sheer bulk and contrived styling were tried to boost sales. **1-2.** The '58 Mark III shared many design cues with the year's Lincolns, including canted tailfins, canted quad headlights, elongated fenders, and heavily sculpted bodysides. Bottom-edge bumper extensions, front and rear, perpetuated the angled look. The convertible was part of a four-model lineup. **3.** For 1959, the Mark IV added this formal sedan and a similar division-window limousine. Some frontal elements anticipated the clean look of 1961, but few will argue that the '59 Continentals were not over-styled. **4.** A reverse-slant opening backlight was just icing on the big, heavy cake.

3

4

Since its debut for 1939, Mercury had shared bodies with other Ford Motor Company cars. Sometimes it appeared to be a fancier Ford; other times it was a lesser Lincoln. All that changed in 1957 when, as part of a corporate reorganization plan, a newly independent Mercury Division was permitted its own bodyshells.

The days of divisional freedom and distinct bodies proved to be brief, but they resulted in some of the most flamboyant Mercs ever: the '57 Turnpike Cruiser and the '58 Park Lane. Gene Bordinat, destined to succeed George Walker as styling vice president, directed Mercury design.

6

7

1. The rear end of this early clay for the 1957 Mercury borrowed liberally from the XM-800, a 1954 show car designed by Elwood Engel and John Najjar. 2. This proposal was an evolution of the 1956 production design. Six-window side glass was somewhat GM-like. 3-4. Swept wheel openings on this clay model were a detail that survived to production. "Lightning-bolt" side trim, first seen on '56 Mercs, wouldn't last. 5. Deeply hooded headlights, bumper-tip "bombs," and a segmented concave grille also came from the XM-800. 6-9. Another Engel/Najjar dream car, the XM-Turnpike Cruiser begun in 1954 and shown in 1956, had more impact on '57 Mercury styling. Canted fins and wedge taillights came from it. A distinctive roof was developed for the production Turnpike Cruiser hardtops.

8

9

For 1957-58, Mercury distilled—and exaggerated—a multitude of design conventions. **1.** The famously eccentric Turnpike Cruiser had arching headlight brows, nacelle bulges to fit the quad lamps, and a retractable backlight. An air intake sat atop each A-pillar. Narrow, elevated side coves that culminated in sharply canted, wedge-shape taillights were common to all series. So were massive bumpers with twin rectangular openings. **2-3.** Lesser models, like the Montclair and Commuter wagon, were more subdued and looked good with dual headlights. **4.** A Convertible Cruiser paced the '57 Indianapolis 500, inspiring showroom replicas. **5.** Quad lamps were a better fit in '58s like this Montclair. **6.** The new Park Lane was space-age gaudy. Note the faux ritzy roof treatment.

1

2

3

4

5

6

GENERAL MOTORS CORPORATION

The first all-new General Motors post-war cars that made their debuts in 1948 and '49 were especially good looking. With front fenders flush with the doors and saucy outrigger rear-fender forms, they bore an uncanny resemblance to Phil Wright's innovative 1933 Pierce Silver Arrow. What's more, the pioneering "hardtop convertible" style seen on 1949 Oldsmobiles, Buicks, and Cadillacs would soon be universally imitated.

But this promising beginning was negated as GM entered the Fifties with the rotund, retrograde 1950 Buick. Stylistically, it was a step backward, yet it embodied everything that GM's styling guru, Harley Earl, held dear. The hood towered above the fenders, cascading onto the fender forms, whose equally large-radius sections waterfalled to the ground, burying the rear wheels. As Paul Wilson astutely observed in his book *Chrome Dreams*, this Buick looked as if it had been modeled not with clay, but with mounds of sand, like a gigantic beach sculpture. But to "Misterl"—as the stylists called him—high hoods implied power, and large-radius forms signaled road-hugging weight and safety-in-size bulk. The look was consistent with Earl's favorite concept cars, the prewar Y-Job and the postwar LeSabre, both of which served him as daily drivers.

As the decade progressed, all other GM cars echoed this philosophy, including the 1953-54 Chevrolets. While not unattractive, their soft, lazy-looking contours were hardly expressions of speed or agility. Compare a '54 Chevy to a '54 Ford—one look will tell you which has the timeworn six and which the sprightlier V-8.

But things began to change with the debut of the 1954 Buicks and Oldsmobiles, good-looking cars whose lowered hoods, clean lines, and taut surfaces looked a lot less bulky and a lot more lively. The vestigial rear fender forms at last disappeared into the bodysides and wheels were rediscovered. On most two-door Buicks, both the front and rear wheels were fully exposed for a more agile look, while some Oldsmobiles featured rakish teardrop-shaped wheel apertures. Other advances included a sporty notched beltline and that miracle of glass bending, the wraparound windshield, which instantly became the *sine qua non* of styling modernity. Both these features were lifted directly from the LeSabre.

These styling trends crystallized in the 1955 "Motoramic" Chevrolet. With its crisp three-box design, notched belt, wraparound windshield, and Ferrari-like grille, it looked like a car with a hot V-8 underhood. Winsome and sized right, this fondly remembered collectible Chevy is arguably GM's best design of the Fifties.

Starting in 1953, there were, of course, two Chevys, the other being the two-place Corvette, conjured up by Earl in response to the imported sports cars dashing about the countryside. Based on a Motorama show car, the Corvette's body was fiberglass, a material that GM Styling was using to replace wood in the building of full-size evaluation models. Despite their rounded contours, the 1953-55 Corvettes were quite attractive, with their wire-mesh headlight covers and toothy grillework. Those headlight covers disappeared in a 1956 redo, the front end assuming a more aggressive attitude while an elliptical body indentation allowed for two-tones, a theme that continued for the rest of the decade.

Beside their production-car assignments, GM designers were involved in creating advanced concepts for the periodic Motorama shows. In the years when the corporation chose to hold them, the public in select cities flocked to the Motoramas, eager to be treated to elaborate stage productions showcasing the "dream car" concepts and GM's then-current product lineup. Ultimately, the shows grew too expensive even for GM. But their presence lingers: Displaying an advanced concept vehicle is the "price of admission" for auto-show exhibitors even today.

As Earl came closer to retirement, he inexplicably chose to revisit the '50 Buick. In developing GM's 1958 cars, large-radius curves were back. While the Chevrolet Impala and Pontiac Bonneville hardtops were attractive enough, the Buicks and Oldsmobiles were dreadful. On the bulked-up Buick, the rear wheels were once again buried and the hood once more rose above the fendertops. And the Oldsmobiles, with their chubby-cheek headlamp forms and bulging sides, were equally bad. Worse yet, their flanks were piled with vast expanses of truly bizarre chromium decoration.

Aghast at these vulgarities, the younger designers, led by future design vice president Chuck Jordan, revolted after spying Virgil Exner's clean-lined, radically finned '57 Plymouths through a factory shipping-yard fence. They scrapped what GM had been planning for 1959 and started over. In an orgy of unleashed creativity, the designers conjured up the wildest cars of the decade. Bat-wing Chevys, wedge-wing Buicks, split-grille Pontiacs, and rocket-tail Cadillacs out-finned upstart Chrysler with a vengeance. Though GM moved quickly away from fins (excepting originator Cadillac), the ponderous forms were gone forever as Bill Mitchell succeeded Earl and the Sixties began.

1953 BUICK

1

3

7

B uick got a new suit as a present for its 50th birthday in '53. While built on the same B and C bodyshells in use since 1950, the golden-anniversary cars were provided with lots of new sheetmetal and trim.

The Buick XP-300 show car of 1951 lent its oval head-lamp/parking-lamp bezels. A toothy "waterfall" grille was continued, but a new bumper design incorporated a 50th-anniversary badge. Sculpting on the hood was widened (allowing for a wider hood emblem). Rear fenders were raised to incorporate free-standing "bullet" taillights.

Studio chief Ned Nickles's personal customized convertible set the pattern for the limited-edtion '53 Skylark. It, in turn, influenced later Buicks.

1. The 1951 XP-300 show car contained a number of Buick styling cues of the Fifties. **2-3.** B- and C-body cars (2 and 3, respectively) seen on July 26, 1950, display several discarded styling and trim suggestions for the early Fifties. **4-6.** In the early months of 1951, Buick designers were trying out various taillight ideas for 1953. **7.** Wide hood sculpting on this January 5, 1951, clay would stay; the loop bumper would not. **8-9.** A '53 or possible '54 B-body update in early 1951.

1. The fabulous Buick Skylark was a limited-production, convertible-only car that, like the Olds Fiesta and Cadillac Eldorado, began life on the show circuit. Skylark sold better for '53 than the other two combined, and helped cement Buick's status as GM's near-luxury make. Its open rear wheelwells and dramatic sweepspear bodyside trim would define the division's styling through 1957. 2. The Super Riviera sedan was a natural evolution of the 1950-52 cars, with similar side trim and roofline. Stacked bullet taillights were new. 3. The toothy grille of the Roadmaster said "Buick" just as clearly as the "VentiPorts." The hood was more dramatically sculpted than before. 4. The Special Riviera hardtop with three portholes, restrained rear-quarter detailing, and a tall fenderline.

3

4

149

With new body shells in the program for 1954, there was a lot that was new about the appearance of that year's Buicks. Larger wraparound windshields, with "dogleg" A-pillars, were instituted across the line. Hoods and beltlines were lowered to the point that on B-body cars, the belt and fenderlines had merged.

Detailing was evolutionary. The grille and front bumper themes were similar to the '53 styles, though the former featured narrower teeth and more of them. Bullet taillights remained, but rear fenders grew low-rise fins.

6

7

8

9

1-2. Buick historians Terry Dunham and Lawrence Gustin have written that the division asked to have its stylists start working on designs for 1954 as early as July 1950, which would have extended the normal design-cycle time. By December 12, 1951, Ned Nickles's Buick Studio had this sedan clay that mixed B- and C-body elements to show for its efforts. **3.** A proposed Roadmaster two-door hardtop snapped on March 18, 1952. The 1952-style grille and front bumper would not last. Neither would the low-cut rear-wheel openings. All 1954 hardtops and convertibles would get fully open wheelwells and checkmark side trim, touches borrowed from the '53 Skylark. The roof style, vertical windshield pillar, and raised cowl intake were all features of the GM C-body also used by Cadillac. **4-5.** A further refinement of the senior-series sedan. Side trim, bumper guards, and the grille still were destined to change. **6.** By August '52, the ultimately accepted grille existed. **7.** Heavy side trim was planned for a time, but deleted. **8-9.** The fine-toothed concave grille and triangular rear-door trim on this B-body mock-up from September 26, 1952, were never used.

151

1

2

152

1-2. The '54 Skylark convertible was an elaboration of the '53 model. Open wheel arches continued, but with deep scoops, some of which were painted red at the factory. The decklid was sculpted and deeply curved, and chrome fins inspired by the Wildcat II Motorama show car were—probably unwisely—tacked onto the fendertops. (Buick stylist Ned Nickles said Harley Earl favored them.) Taillights were shrouded ovoids. The hood ornament was gun-sight style, and badging was new. Despite the Skylark's luxo looks and a reduced price, buyers this year were more taken with the similar Cadillac Eldorado, so 1954 was the swan song for the uplevel Skylark, as Buick pursued cars with volume potential. **3.** A revived Century series included Buick's first all-steel station wagon in its ranks. The dipping and rising beltline added interest. **4.** The Roadmaster convertible shows off the new thin-bar grille beneath the lowered hood.

3

4

With Buick in the thick of a tough battle for third place in industry sales, any edge was crucial. Ned Nickles, assistant chief designer Homer LaGassey, and their styling staff handled the appearance part.

The chrome-tooth grille, a Buick staple, was dropped for a mesh surface. Heavy chrome taillight bezels capped the rear of all '55s. Four-door hardtop styling came to the B-body lines.

1-2. Compared to these October 14, 1953, B-body models, the grille opening on production '55 Buicks would be larger. **3.** The headlight rims and grille on this April '54 C-body mock-up would be changed. **4.** A mesh grille, toned-down floating bar, and round "portholes" marked '55s like this Special.

1956 BUICK

The final year on the 1954-vintage bodies called for another facelift. A new grille, a pointed hood with revised sculpting, and open rear wheelwells on all models did the trick. Specials and Centurys had thick chrome head- and taillight surrounds. Roadmasters had lamps edged in narrow bands of brightwork. The Super and Roadmaster lines added four-door hardtops.

1-4. Key detail changes on the 1956 facelift took place between September (1, 2) and December (3, 4) 1954. 5. A Roadmaster shows off 1956's reshaped bumpers and parking lights that projected from the fenders.

1957 BUICK

To some eyes—including a few around General Motors itself—the 1957 Buicks were a backward step. "Suddenly, it's 1949," said one wag, paraphrasing the '57 Plymouth advertising slogan. Doubters pointed to divided rear windows and plump roofs that showed a lot of crown in profile.

In other areas, though, the '57 design took the familiar Buick look and made it sleeker. The hood slipped beneath the height of the fendertops. Vertical grille teeth returned, and side sweepspears now were paint-filled. Buick also joined in the nascent market for hardtop station wagons with a pair of four-door models.

1. The 1957 C-body Super and Road-master hardtops got a new roof design with back-slanting windshield posts and forward-angled rear-roof pillars—the latter a touch that had been used on 1953-54 Chevrolets and Pontiacs. 2-4. This Roadmaster mock-up shown on September 16, 1955, sports fender-top ornaments and side trim that extends into the taillight housing, details that ultimately didn't go into production. The three-piece backlight was produced, but Roadmaster buyers could opt for an undivided rear window. 5. This B-body model shows the grille variations considered before an "electric shaver" style was settled upon. 6-9. A comparison of photos shows how much detail work was done to the B-body design between May 19 (7, 8) and September 16, 1955 (6, 9). Sedans and hardtops had the same essential roof with longitudinal ribs that continued through the decklid.

Buick enjoyed strong sales for model years 1954 to '56. For '57, the division retained much of its visual character, but some styling changes didn't sit well with shoppers, and helped send Buick production from third to fourth industrywide. **1-2.** The Series 75 Roadmaster represented the tip-top of the Buick line; seen here are hardtops in two- and four-door guise. The familiarly contoured bodyside sweepspears were retained. So were the bold wheel arches and portholes. Changes included a sharply angled A-pillar, which gave added emphasis to the ferocious wrap of the windshield. Sculptured hoods and fussy decks were abandoned. **3.** Heavily chromed fins were hard to ignore, but what set the teeth of many shoppers on edge was the divided, three-piece backlight, seen here on the "performance" Buick, the Century. Although not mandatory on all Buicks, the treatment was deemed old-fashioned by many. **4.** Narrower grillework imparted a road-hugging stance, as on this Century convertible. **5.** Few wagons looked as slick or dynamic as the hardtop Century Caballero. Longitudinal roof indents recalled the Chevy Nomad. Note the shapely glass areas.

1

2

3

4

5

1958 BUICK

Those who might have worried about Buick's design direction in 1957 would not have rested any easier in '58. Sheer bulk, in sheetmetal and in chrome, was the order of the day.

After years of lowering the hood to the point that it was no higher than the fendertops, the '58 Buicks reverted to a tall dome with a blunt front. With it came the return of a distinct beltline on the costlier C-body cars, another feature that had been fading as Detroit designs increasingly strove for lowness. Radiused rear-wheel cutouts were abandoned, giving the rear quarters a heavy profile.

Buick's trademark "Venti-Ports" were removed, but there barely would have been room for them anyway amid all the other bright-work. The bodyside sweep-spear remained, but was nearly buried under a huge chrome projectile on the rear half of most models.

A new Limited series led the lineup, but seemed less chrome-bound in places. More body color showed through on the hash-mark-decorated sides, and tail-light bezels weren't as big.

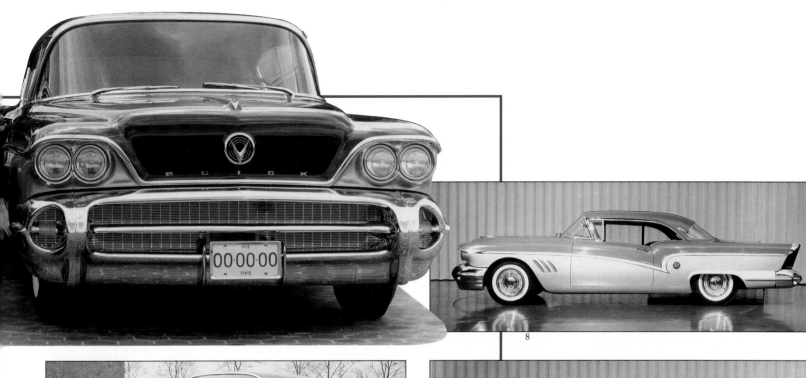

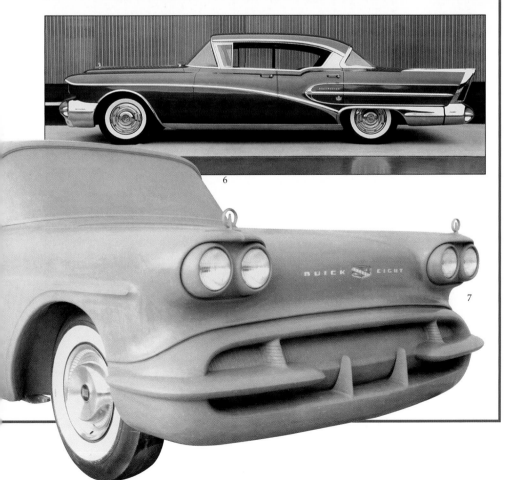

8

9

5

6

7

1. The ready-for-market 1957 Buick is compared to the developing 1958 design in September 1956. **2-4.** In January 1957, trim and two-toning possibilities for the larger C-body cars were under consideration. Though badged Roadmaster, the mock-up in pictures 2 and 3 has rear-quarter and taillight trim similar to what would be used on the new top-of-the-line Limited series. **5.** By April 4, 1957, side trim was nearing its final form, and the complicated "Fashion-Aire Dynastar Grille" design was emerging. **6.** Less than two months earlier, rear-quarter brightwork had been a bit more toned down. **7.** Stylists made quite a leap to the 1958 Buick's tall hood and 160-piece grille. On January 8, 1956, they were developing this face. **8-9.** Exactly one year later, these Special (8) and Century (9) trim ideas were reviewed.

1

2

Economic recession and increasing buyer interest in small cars meant that Buick took its lumps for 1958. Production fell to fifth overall. **1-2.** The Limited was Buick's new top-of-the-line series, and rivaled Cadillac in price. Like other Buicks, it sported quad headlamps beneath heavy brows; a wide, incredibly complex grille comprised of 160 four-faceted chrome squares; and side-pod parking lights. Specific Limited brightwork included completely gratuitous rear-quarter

hash marks. **3.** Buick hoods, which had been getting lower in recent years, humped upward for '58, as seen on this Series 75 Roadmaster convertible. The change contributed to an impression of unwarranted heft. Side cove treatment was much more dense here than on the Limited, and was even less pleasing than that model's hash marks. **4.** The Caballero hardtop wagon returned, but what had been rakish now was chunky. **5.** Heavily chromed fins continued, flanking a twin-bar bumper, as on this Super. All divided rear windows were dropped.

All it took was a look at the '57 Plymouths and the minds of GM stylists started racing ahead two model years. They knew the 1959 designs on which they were already working were going to be hopelessly outmoded.

Thus began a crash program in each studio to dump Harley Earl's preference for hulking roundness. In its place emerged low, wide, sharp-edged styles—some with flaring fins, all with lots of glass.

The corporation also took the cost-saving opportunity to put its five car lines on a single body. Buick set the tone. Its cowl, windshield, and front-door dimensions were adopted by the others.

1-2. This Buick clay from October 1956 was typical of early plans for the '59s. Its face was inspired by the 1951 LeSabre show car. **3-4.** A more-linear concept from February '57 was still beset by thick contours. **5-6.** Another late-1956 clay clearly derived from the '58 theme.

2

4

6

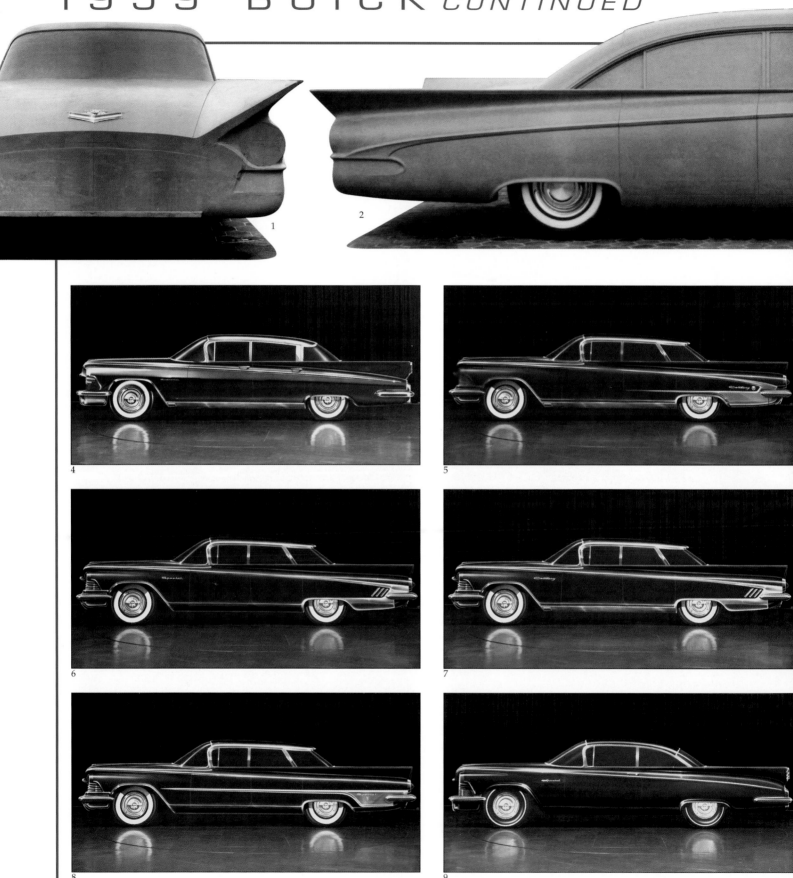

1-3. April 29, 1957: A clay model for a six-window hardtop sedan displays much of what would become the '59 look, though the windshield A-pillar, grille, and front bumper would be changed. **4-9.** A series of full-size profile renderings from October '57 tries out various designs for hardtop roofs and side trim. All the familiar Buick series names seen here were swept away in '59. **10.** A June 1957 hardtop station wagon clay (with Oldsmobile styling on the left side). **11.** This twin-grille idea was in the works on October 22, 1957. **12.** A more acceptable front had already emerged, though.

167

1

2

168

GM forfeited its styling leadership to Chrysler Corporation after middecade, and could not respond with a low and long look of its own until the '59 model year. **1.** The crisp Electra 225 convertible was light years removed from the '58 Buicks. Although hyperlong at 225.9 inches (on a 126.3-inch wheelbase), the Electra—for all of its numerous excesses—was a step that GM and Buick needed to take. **2.** An Electra four-door hardtop, showing the canted headlights and fendertops that echoed the sweep of the fins. **3.** The LeSabre sedan displayed enormous glass area and beautifully slender roof pillars. **4.** Critics carped about the expansive deck and winglike fins.

3

4

Finally freed from the obligations of naval service, William L. Mitchell returned to his pre-World War II job: designing Cadillacs. He resumed his role as studio chief in time to direct work on the fully redone 1950 models.

The '50s came in the wake of the division's first all-new postwar cars of 1948-49, which were styled under

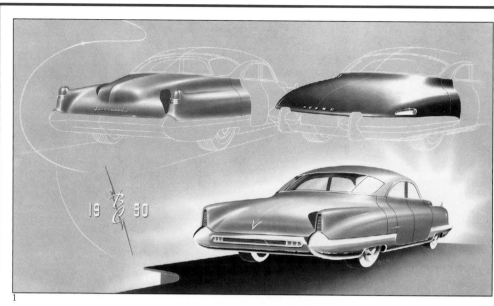

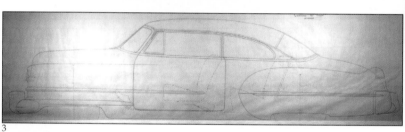

the auspices of Franklin Hershey and assistant Ned Nickles. Sizing up these late-Forties cars for himself, Mitchell apparently didn't like them. He felt they were too tall and narrow. With the studio back under his command, Mitchell and company turned out cars that were lower, wider, and more "important" looking.

Mitchell had a clean sheet on which to execute his ideas. A new group of Fisher bodies was approved for 1950, and Cadillac based its cars on them: B-body for

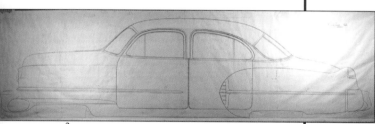

1. A July 1947 sketch for the proposed 1950 cars explores how decklid and fender changes could be used to differentiate Cadillacs and Buicks built on shared bodies. **2-3.** Dimensional drawings from the same month for a Series 62 sedan (2) and Series 61 coupe (3). The "florentine curve" rear-roof pillar would be adopted for both styles, but the doors of four-door sedans would be altered. **4.** This profile rendering proposed using a then-trendy straight-through fenderline. **5-7.** A clay model from August '47. The "cathedral"-style headlamps showed up in many early drawings and models for the 1950 Cadillac.

5

6

7

the lowest-cost Series 61, C-body for most others, and a stretched D-body for the first all-new Caddy limousines and formal sedans since the war.

Mitchell did keep one key Hershey-era detail. The 1948-49 cars featured rear-fender "bumps" that would grow into a styling icon of the Fifties—the tailfin.

4

5

6

7

8

1-3. By February 1948, the design concept had moved away from pontoon rear fenders and adopted a "six-window" roof for the C-body sedan. Rectangular wraparound taillights would have been a departure from the wedge-shaped lamps in the fins on 1948 and '49 cars. **4-8.** As in previous years, a fastback coupe was proposed for the entry-level Series 61. Developments on the ultimately discarded body style are shown in February (4, 5), May (6, 7), and November 1948 (8). **9.** Fin alternatives—likely for a '51 update—as seen on May 26, 1949.

9

1

1-2. The B-body Series 61 was the price-leader Cadillac for 1950. Although a hardtop coupe was available, the four-door sedan (shown) was the production leader. The upswept taillights first used in 1948 were still modest, but undeniably more noticeable—a bellwether of Cad styling to come. The vertical faux intake vents aft the centerline also were refined. **3.** The Series 61 hardtop coupe had what GM design chief Harley Earl called a "florentine roof," which flowed back in an unbroken, chrome-accented line. All Caddys now had one-piece windshields.

2

3

175

1952 CADILLAC

Aside from riding herd on General Motors's styling operation, Harley Earl also owned his own industrial design firm. In 1949, after he had produced a facelift for the 1951 Cadillac, Bill Mitchell was pursuaded by Earl to leave GM for a time to manage his boss's design house.

Mitchell's place at Cadillac was taken by Joe Schemansky, his assistant chief designer. The cascading contours—roof, to beltline, to fenderline—continued unaltered, but details were tweaked. Winged emblems (gold-toned, no less) newly flanked the grille, and exhaust outlets were added to the rear bumper.

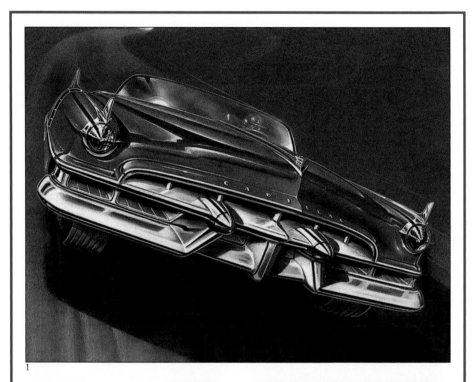

1

2

3

4

1. A February 1950 sketch suggests a grille with integral canted bumper guards. **2-3.** Trim ideas being evaluated on July 26, 1950. This sedan is a B-body Series 61, which Cadillac ultimately discontinued after '51. **4.** Side trim on Series 62s, like the two-door hardtop, was unchanged from 1951. **5.** This convertible's gold hood "V" signified Caddy's 50th anniversary.

5

The final facelift of the body instituted for 1950 was prepared for '53. It was completed under Ed Glowacke, who took over the Cadillac Studio in 1951.

The grille-mounted parking lights moved aside for heavy bumper bombs. At the top of the price list sat a new Eldorado convertible with a wrapped windshield and dipped beltline.

1

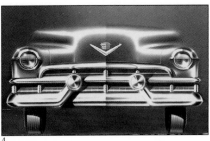
2

3

4

5

6

1-4. Prospects for the carefully evolved Cadillac "face" from April 1950 (1, 2) and November 1951 (3, 4). **5.** Big new bumper bombs on the '53s displaced the parking lights, which moved beneath the headlights, themselves more hooded than before. Hardtops now had a one-piece backlight. **6.** Eldorados sported a wraparound windshield and a color-keyed metal top boot.

1954 CADILLAC

One of Cadillac's market strengths had been the consistency of its look. Certain persistent and carefully nurtured styling touches created a Caddy "look" that maintained a brand image from year to year. The all-new '54 line was a perfect example.

The general grille outline developed in the late Forties was continued, but the few, heavy crossed bars of recent years were replaced by a

1

2

3

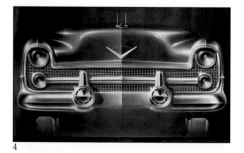

4

5

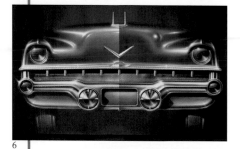

6

7

tighter eggcrate pattern. The prominent "prow" hood sat lower and flatter. Headlamp hoods were now built into the fenders, not just the chrome trim rings. Wraparound windshields were standardized. Fins and taillamps were made larger.

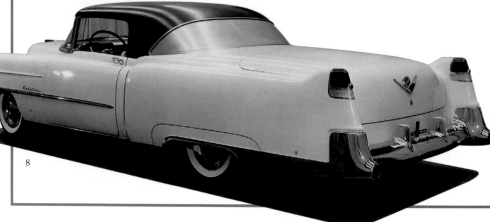

8

9

10

11

12

1. A clay model from March 5, 1953, features a raised grille center and rectangular parking lights not seen on the production '54 models. **2-7.** More possible mid-Fifties grille treatments from early March 1953. **8.** This odd short-roof coupe idea was photographed on February 6, 1953. **9-10.** To effect a price cut, the 1954 Eldorado shared its body with the Series 62 convertible, but used bold, ribbed quarter-panel trim and a metal boot. **11.** Sixty Special long-wheelbase sedans continued to use hash-mark trim. **12.** A Series 62 sedan had a far shorter deck.

W ith new bodies instituted for 1954, facelifts were in order for the next two model years. Grille textures were altered, bodyside "scoops" were shortened, and four-door hardtops were added in '56.

The Eldorado garnered added distinction in these years. Tall blade fins and twin-tube taillights—a preview of future Cadillac styling—came in for 1955. Then, in 1956, the line was expanded with the addition of a two-door hardtop.

1. The 1954 La Espada show car's fins predicted the rear treatment of the 1955-56 Eldorado. **2.** Bits of the La Espada look were eyed for the '56 production-car facelift, too. **3.** Oval bumper-tip exhaust outlets would be adopted for most '56s. **4.** The forward bodyside spear linked up with the dummy side vent on the '55s. **5.** A Seville hardtop made Eldorado a two-car series in '56. **6.** The same year saw the first Sedan de Ville four-door hardtop.

A styling team that consisted of chief designer Ed Glowacke, assistant Bob Scheelk, Dave Holls, Ned Walters, and Ron Hill designed a completely new line of Cadillacs for 1957. Not only were the "standard" models completely redesigned, but the Eldorados continued with rear styling all their own and an ultraexclusive Eldorado Brougham joined the line.

A new X-frame chassis helped lower the C-body cars by three inches. Blade fins and round taillights for the regular models were derived from the 1955-56 Eldorados. The '57 Eldo Seville hardtop and Biarritz convertible shared a new sloping deck, freestanding "shark fins," and heavy nerf-style rear bumpers.

1-3. The rear-angled fins of this April 21, 1955, clay would have to wait. Side grilles were used in '57, but in a toned-down form. **4-5.** A month later, the design—now with forward-leaning fins—was closer to production form. The divided rear window wouldn't be adopted by Cadillac, wisely, it turned out. **6-7.** Alternate trim ideas for the Series 62 and Sixty Special were modeled in October '55. **8.** Only details separate this December 1955 mock-up from production readiness.

New interiors, cruciform frames, and all-new sheetmetal marked the 1957 Cadillacs. These were radically freshened cars, but because the front ends leaned back and the rear fins leaned forward, many dealers and shoppers thought they looked short. **1.** For '57, the Fleetwood Sixty Special switched from four-door sedan to four-door hardtop configuration. Caddy's hooded headlamps now looked like languid eyelids. **2-3.** The Series 62 was available in a variety of body and trim variations, including plusher De Ville and Eldorado models. The 62 hardtop sedan (2) looked sleek sans roof pillar, and with the severely wrapped windshield and backlight. This ragtop (3) shows the twin-pod taillight/backup light combo. **4-5.** The Eldorado, whether a Seville hardtop or Biarritz convertible, had a unique, fallaway deck flanked by dramatically outthrust fins. The design was the work of 23-year-old junior stylist Ron Hill.

4

5

The 1954 Motorama Park Avenue begat the 1955 Motorama Eldorado Brougham, which begat the 1957 showroom Brougham, which Cadillac hoped would make free-spending customers forget the Continental Mark II.

When Harley Earl saw that serious shoppers were drawn to his custom four-door show cars, the styling czar and Cadillac management figured they had hit on the formula for a rival to Ford Motor Company's upcoming ultraluxury car. They packed the Brougham with styling, technical, and comfort advances for a price that assured exclusivity.

The 1957 Eldo Brougham was among the first U.S. cars with quad headlights. It was barely touched for '58, then replaced for 1959-60 with looks that foreshadowed early Sixties Caddys.

6

7

8

9

1. The Eldorado Brougham that made it into the hands of a very few well-to-do buyers in 1957 had its start in this 1955 show car of the same name. **2-4.** In late January 1955, the developing production-car design featured conventional dual headlights and a roof design adapted from yet another Cadillac dream car, 1954's El Camino coupe. Rear styling at the time was a somewhat exaggerated version of the production Eldorado convertible's tail. **5.** By August 17, 1955, a new roof and side trim—both close to final form—were on a mock-up. Quad headlights and rubber bumper tips were still in the offing. **6-7.** Air suspenion, sumptuous upholstery, power conveniences, front and rear vanity cases—even a set of magnetized tumblers—helped push the price of a new Eldorado Brougham to more than $13,000 in 1957. The brushed stainless-steel roof was a touch particularly favored by General Motors styling boss Harley Earl. **8-9.** New color choices and slight interior modifications distinguished these '58 Broughams from the 1957 model. The 400 built for '57 were followed by 304 of the '58s.

1958 CADILLAC

With its 1958 facelift, Cadillac addressed a rare criticism: Some people thought its 1957 cars looked too short. The tailfins were given a rearward rake, and the division even added a second type of Series 62 hardtop sedan with an extended deck. The gullwing front bumper motif was dropped, but bumper bombs survived at the ends of a new full-width grille design cooked up in a special studio run by Pete Wozena. The traditional eggcrate look was dumped, too, replaced by 80 little chrome projectiles. Taillight lenses were now hooded, and four-door models added C-pillar vent windows.

1. The 1954 El Camino show coupe provided an accurate forecast of the 1958 Cadillac look. **2.** The '58 facelift, with its new grille and quad headlamps, as of February 6, 1956. **3.** Ron Hill, who was chiefly responsible for the rear design of the '57 Eldorado, made this sketch for the '58 Caddy tail. **4.** An early July '56 clay with the fin, taillight, and bumper-tip styles that would reach production. **5.** Later that month, the studio was still open to considering a tail-lamp pod with a "bullet" lens. **6.** Hill, then the junior member of the Caddy design staff, drew this twin-pod variation of the concept. **7-8.** Until Ed Glowacke scaled back the amount of decoration, the Sixty Special virtually oozed chrome. **9.** The '57 and '58 mock-up in September 1956.

189

1

1. For 1958, a small window replaced the metal C-pillar extension that kicked up from the rear doors of the '57s. This is a Fleetwood Sixty Special. Cadillac Studio design chief Ed Glowacke removed much of the proposed '58 brightwork before production. Hash marks; "V"s on the outside of the fins; and thick, horizontal chrome strips aft of the front wheel arches were dumped, but chromed rocker panels, reverse "C"s above the front-bumper wraparounds (which replaced the aforementioned horizontal strips), and a sea of chrome on the lower rear quarters remained. Although not completely irrational on a Caddy, the decoration nevertheless was emblematic of the overwrought nature of corporate styling for 1958. **2-9.** Promotional photos of other cars in the '58 Cadillac line reveal variations in trim and body style. In number order, these are the Series 62 convertible, Series 62 Coupe de Ville, Series 62 hardtop coupe, Sedan de Ville four-door hardtop, 62 long-deck hardtop sedan, 62 standard hardtop sedan, Eldorado Seville hardtop coupe, and majestic Series 75 limousine. The last rode a prodigious 149.8-inch wheelbase, was 237.1 inches long overall, and seated nine.

2

3

4

5

6

7

8

9

1 9 5 9   C A D I L L A C

For good or for ill, Cadillac created a legendary design for 1959. Out of frantic efforts to abruptly change its design course to keep from being outshone by Chrysler, the Cadillac Studio produced the tallest fins ever mounted on a production car. The tastefulness of the design has been debated ever since, but over time, the '59 Caddy has become a pop-culture cliché for the nostalgic notion of the "Fabulous Fifties."

Staff designer Dave Holls took the lead role in the '59 Cadillac design, especially the rudderlike fins to which long nacelles that held the bullet-style taillamps were affixed. When Ed Glowacke's stylists abandoned a tall hood that would have been more at home on the '56 Caddy, they replaced it with a flatter, beveled hood with the look of the La Espada/El Camino show cars. Rear-bumper pods, conceived as exhaust outlets, held the back-up lights.

One casualty of GM's '59 body sharing was a distinct Eldorado. Specialized rear sheetmetal was deemed too costly, so Eldos resumed using the Series 62 tail.

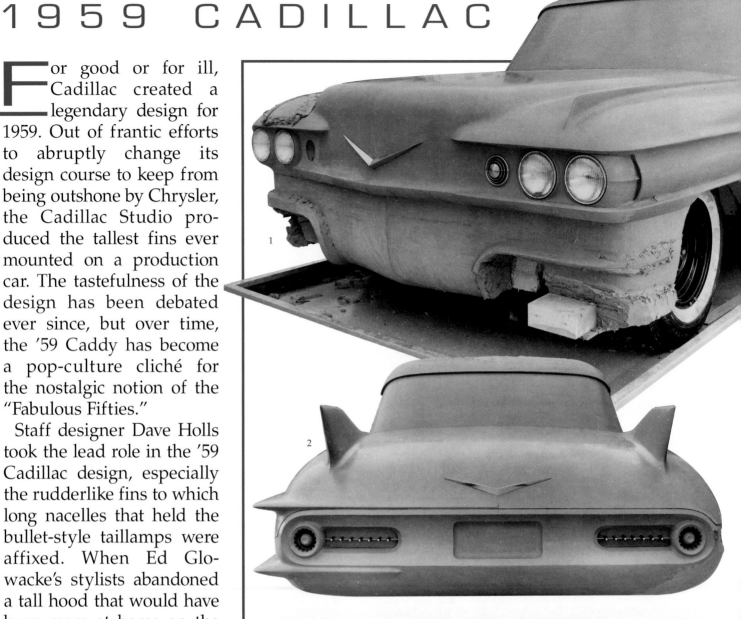

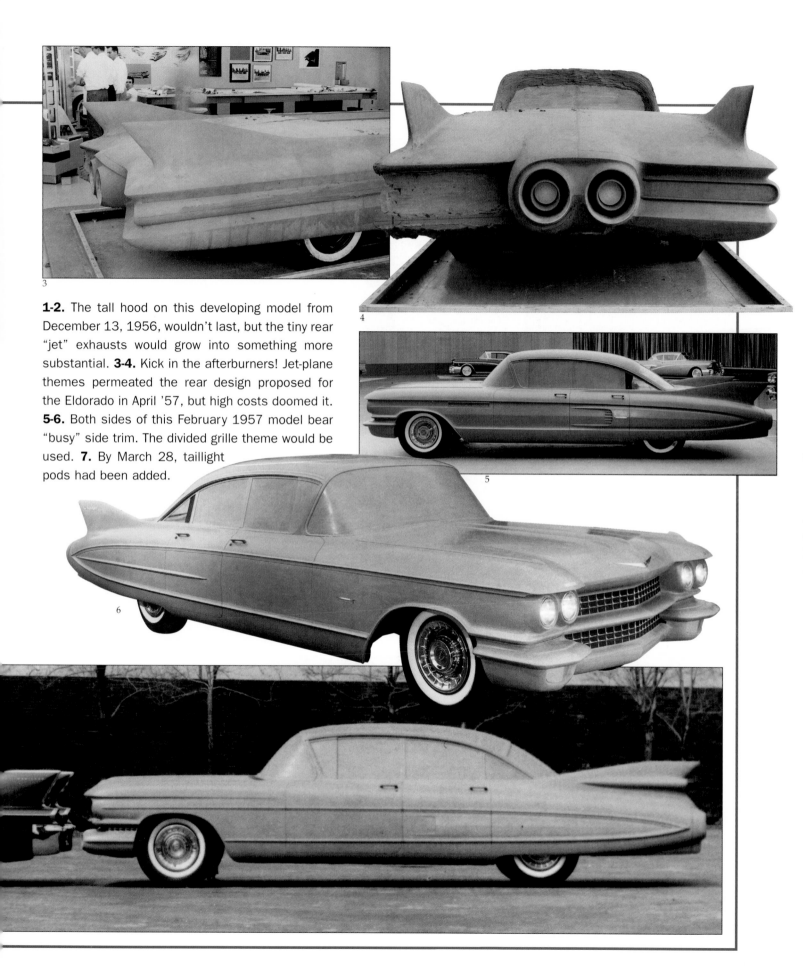

1-2. The tall hood on this developing model from December 13, 1956, wouldn't last, but the tiny rear "jet" exhausts would grow into something more substantial. **3-4.** Kick in the afterburners! Jet-plane themes permeated the rear design proposed for the Eldorado in April '57, but high costs doomed it. **5-6.** Both sides of this February 1957 model bear "busy" side trim. The divided grille theme would be used. **7.** By March 28, taillight pods had been added.

1

2

The '59 Cadillac is best known for its extroverted fins, but the most novel design aspect involves the doors: Because GM wanted to cut costs even as it raced to regain design leadership from Chrysler Corporation, all GM lines had to share Buick's front doors. The taper of those doors dictated the bodyline sweep of the '59 Caddy—one of that flamboyant car's most pleasing aspects. **1-2.** The Series 62 convertible coupe had an aircraft-inspired, straight-through bodyline, as well as a welcome return to sanity vis-à-vis bodyside trim. The car's primary designer, Dave Holls, maintained the aviation theme with the nacelle pods for the taillamps and "exhaust-port" back-up lights. **3.** The fabulous roofline and deck of the Series 62 hardtop sedan helped move 23,000 units.

3

1952-54 CHEVROLET

From a design standpoint, the 1952 Chevrolet offered nothing but a trim shuffle from the '51 model, which itself was an update of the first new postwar design of 1949-50. The 1953 and '54 Chevys were different to be sure, but in an evolutionary way.

Aside from revised side trim, the '52s added five teeth and wider parking lights

to the 1951 grille design. The year also saw the last use of the fastback body style that had been all the rage in the Forties.

Though the '53s retained the aging separate-fender look in the rear, those fenders were now taller and squarer, and ended in stylized taillights. The windshield became a one-piece unit, and hardtops went to

2

3

1-3. Though Chevrolets were built on the corporate A-body, the fenderline on these '52 two- and four-door sedan proposals from July 10, 1949, shows influences of the modified B-body used on certain early Fifties Buicks and Oldsmobiles. 4-5. This concurrent upper-level convertible mock-up displays grille teeth similar to those adopted for 1952 production. The single-pane windshield would have to wait, though. 6-7. Inklings of the '53 Chevy look were on this September 2, 1949, clay. Note the tall rear fenders, square-edged rear-door cut, and crease trailing from the headlights.

6

7

reverse-angle rear pillars. Facelifted '54s got a wider grille and almond-shaped taillight housings.

Styling for the 1952-54 cars was directed by studio chief Ed Glowacke, a veteran designer esteemed by GM styling vice president Harley Earl and his second-in-command, Bill Mitchell.

1. By April 6, 1950, the reverse-slant hardtop roof that would reach production was on a clay model. Neither the divided rear window nor the 1952-style taillights would be used, though. **2.** Once-popular fastback sedans were on the wane when this clay for a still-born '53 version was fashioned. (Note the left-side Pontiac fender.) **3.** The final '53 hardtop mock-up trimmed as a Bel Air, Chevy's new top-line series.

4. Separate rear fenders were beginning to make Chevrolets like the Fleetline DeLuxe look dated by 1952. Though still working with the 1949 body, Chevy designers under Ed Glowacke achieved reasonable freshness. Retooled hood and trunk emblems were created, and bright-work was added to the grille and rear fenders. The '52 DeLuxe two-door was Chevy's only Fleetline offering for the model year. The fastback was a rakish car, particularly with the aftermarket sun visor, but the body style had fallen from favor with buyers. **5.** One reason for the decline of fastbacks in the early Fifties was the ascendency of hardtop coupes, like Chevy's '52 Styleline DeLuxe Bel Air.

4

5

1

2

3

4

The new-looking 1953-54 Chevys still were evolved from the '49s. They also were the last to run with only the "Stovebolt Six," as all Chevys had since 1929. **1-2.** The 1953 Bel Air sedan and convertible, with more bodyside brightwork, rear-fender color inserts, and newly raised taillights. **3-5.** Bel Airs galore from '54: four-door sedan, ragtop, and two-door hardtop. Revisions touched the wheel covers, grille, front bumper, and taillamps.

5

The first-generation Chevrolet Corvette of 1953-55 was a classic bit of Harley Earl automotive fantasy. It even made its debut as a "dream car" in the 1953 edition of General Motors's periodic Motorama exhibitions.

The GM styling chief envisioned an American car to compete with the European sports cars—primarily British—that were gaining a U.S. following in the early Fifties. In fact, in its dimensions and layout, the Corvette was quite similar to the iconic Jaguar XK-120. However, details like a wraparound windshield (from Earl's 1951 LeSabre show car) and jet-pod taillight housings were distinctly Yank in their exuberance.

After its 1953 debut, the Corvette was left alone for '54. Harley Earl wanted to spruce it up for 1955, but slow sales made GM bosses leery of spending additional money on the two-seat sports car. **1.** Proposals for '55 included a hood scoop, Ferarri-like grille, and fake side vents. **2.** A new decklid cove was likewise vetoed.

3

4

3-5. Only 700 Corvettes were built for 1955, and they looked virtually identical to the 1953-54 models. Bodies were slightly smoother, though, and thinner in section. New colors appeared outside (this is Gypsy Red) and inside. Fit and finish were tighter. The big news was underhood, where a special version of Ed Cole's Turbo-Fire V-8—noted by an exaggerated "V" in the body-side script—developed 195 bhp.

5

Chevrolet experienced an amazing transformation in 1955. Low, clean styling and a sizzling little V-8 engine made a jaunty *bon vivant* out of a prim dowager.

Stylists under new studio head Clare MacKichan produced a slab-sided design with a dipped beltline and a broad hood that flattened down to almost fender height. MacKichan's boss, Harley Earl, was a key proponent of the car's rectangular eggcrate grille; some thought it too narrow, but he liked its Ferrari connotations.

A new model for the year was the Nomad station wagon. It featured a rakish two-door roof penned by Carl Renner.

4

1-3. A very complete mock-up of a '55 Chevy Two-Ten four-door sedan as photographed on May 20, 1953. Apart from side trim and a grille that looks like a wider version of the '53 production unit, it is close to the final design. 4-6. Early in the '55 styling cycle, ideas for a special "executive coupe" were floated. These full-size renderings of a three-passenger car called the Grand Prix date from November 3, 1952. 7-8. By January '55, the styling staff had prepared this more-practical—but ultimately abandoned—expression of the idea.

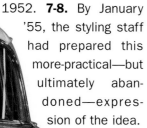

5

6

7

8

1

2

1. The Bel Air convertible showed the clean, lowered nature of the '55 redesign, from eggcrate grille to handsome "finlets." 2. Clare MacKichan and Carl Renner came up with the sleek "sport wagon" dubbed Nomad, which began as a Corvette concept in '54. 3. The "regular" Bel Air wagon carried on the simple grace of the sedans and coupes. 4. A Bel Air hardtop sport coupe, with smart two-toning, well-placed chrome accents, beltline dip, and hooded headlamps. 5. The midrange Two-Ten Delray club coupe featured all-vinyl upholstery. All '55s rode a 115-inch wheelbase.

3

4

5

1

Even after a spectacular record sales year—which 1955 most certainly was—automakers in the Fifties had to come out with something novel the following season. Hence, the substantially facelifted 1956 Chevrolet.

The division lavished $40 million on new styling for '56. Most notable of the new features was a full-width grille, which addressed complaints about the '55 design. The hood now came to a slight point at the center, front fendertops were flattened for more of a Cadillac look, and big sculpted bezels held small "bullet" taillights.

Side trim grew more exaggerated, allowing for splashier two-tone paint schemes. Four-door hardtops appeared with a roof reminiscent of the 1950-52 two-door style.

2

3

4

5

6

1. Four-door hardtops joined the '56 Chevy line, but not with this Buick/Olds-style rear window. **2-6.** Models from May 1954 explore side-trim, bumper, headlight, and wheel-opening variations. **7.** In early August '54, a version of the 1955-style grille was still in place. **8.** By mid October, though, a major change had occurred. **9-10.** Between October 14 (9) and November 30 (10), Bel Air side trim was resolved. **11-12.** Variants of these paint and trim patterns were used on lesser '56s.

7

8

9

10

11

12

1

2

3

1. The '56 Bel Air sport coupe with new swept wheel arches, wider grille, enlarged parking lights, and bolder side trim. The hood "V" meant a V-8. **2.** The Nomad's look got more in line with that of the other Bel Airs in '56. **3.** Four-door hardtops were added as a Two-Ten and this Bel Air. The fuel filler hid behind the left taillamp housing. **4-5.** Two-Ten (4) and Bel Air (5) four-door sedans show the variety of two-tone paint patterns available.

4

5

All signs pointed to the demise of the Chevrolet Corvette after 1955. Even with the addition of V-8 power, sales of the fiberglass-bodied sports car were abysmal. But when Ford introduced the Thunderbird, Chevy found new resolve to stay in the two-seater market.

Those at General Motors who believed in the 'Vette banded together to make it better both in engineering and in styling. Zora Arkus-Duntov took care of the former; Harley Earl and his styling staff handled the latter.

For '56, the essential sweep of the fenderline remained intact, but stylists looked to one of the day's greatest sports cars, the Mercedes-Benz 300SL, for the new design's forward-thrusting headlamps and twin hood windsplits. A toothy grille was retained, but rear fenders shed the gimmicky taillight pods. Bodysides added a concave cove taken from Carl Renner's '55 LaSalle II show car.

1

2

3

4

5

6

The pictures on these pages are a collection of Corvette styling prospects that were photographed on February 1, 1955. **1-2.** As details of the 1956 'Vette were nearing completion, this more-radical style was being pitched for 1957. In profile, it is very much like the LaSalle II roadster drawn up by Carl Renner for the 1955 Motorama shows. The grille and "bullet-nose" blade bumper differ from the show car's design, though. **3-4.** With the deadline for the '56 design looming, Chevy honchos were asked to consider a design featuring short coves in the front and rear fenders. **5-6.** The other side of the model sported a single long cove that would be adopted. Racy side exhaust ports didn't make production.

1

2

Not only did the 1956-57 Corvette have new styling by Harley Earl and Chevy studio chief Clare MacKichan (using molds that were essentially the same as for 1953-55), but, for '57, it picked up a fuel-injected V-8 that delivered 283 bhp—an increase of 43 over the top engine of 1956. **1.** Dramatic side coves that extended well into the doors could be body colored, or go two-tone. The '56s and '57s looked virtually identical, though only the '57s could be had with the injected engine, announced in script in the coves. This generation was more rounded at the rear, eschewing the Buck Rogers taillight pods of 1953-55 for smart, faired-in units. The deck appeared hunkier and more unified than before. **2.** Headlights thrust forward, and the hood had aggressive twin bulges that signaled the 'Vette's graduation to true sports car. Fendertop scoops, though, weren't functional. **3.** No-nonsense monochrome, with simple hubcaps and a removable hardtop.

3

Stylists in Clare MacKichan's Chevrolet Production Studio faced a tough challenge for 1957. They had to make a two-year-old body look fresh compared with the all-new designs from rivals Ford and Plymouth.

A new cowl—an expensive change to make for the final year of an "aging" design—let the hood be flattened even further than before. In front, a hefty "grinning" bumper hung below a mesh grille and chrome bar to hold parking lights and the Chevy emblem. Out back, the '57s truly became "finny" with severely pointed fender tips. Taillights dropped to just above the bumper ends.

3

4

6

7

1-2. In early May 1954, as the '56 design was progressing, this concept emerged. Its broad grille and substantial bumper with "bombs" at the ends turned into the 1957 Chevy face. **3.** A mock-up from August 3, 1955, with pointed chrome bumper guards and four front-fender chevrons, both of which would be altered. **4-5.** Two-Tens were to have a single arc of bright trim, an idea that persisted almost to the start of production. **6-7.** Overhand bumper guards were nixed.

5

1

2

3

Chevy was in the third and final year of this body generation for '57, and changes seemed more calculated than natural. **1-2.** The Bel Air hardtop coupe and convertible display the hard-to-miss twin hood windsplits, bisected grille with Caddy-like "Dagmars" in the bumper, ribbed-aluminum rear-quarter trim inserts, more-pronounced headlight hoods, and fender chevrons. At the rear, dramatically lowered taillights sat below emphatic fins that, to some eyes, threw off the balance of the overall design. **3.** Though the Bel Air four-door sedan wasn't flashy, it seemed less tail heavy than the hardtop coupe and ragtop.

1958 CORVETTE

All constraints aside, Chevrolet stylists would have preferred for the 1958 Corvette to look more like an Oldsmobile show car than a bulked-up version of the 1956-57 'Vette. But with engineering help stretched too thin on other projects, designers had to abandon

plans of turning the 1956 Golden Rocket Motorama car into the new Corvette.

Wheelbase held at 102 inches, but the '58 grew longer and wider. New quad headlights sat above dummy intakes that flanked the narrowed grille cavity. Filler panels trailing three chrome spears sat in each side cove. Simulated hood louvers and decklid brightwork were added, too.

1. An early version of the '58 Corvette's side-cove filler panels showed up on this August '56 clay model. **2.** The previous January, a honeycomb-mesh grille was under consideration. **3.** The Corvette's "traditional" grille teeth were back in place by February 23. **4.** Some sports-car purists decried touches like the twin decklid trim strips. **5.** A 'Vette face and the body of the Olds Golden Rocket coupe.

6

7

Corvette became glitzier for 1958, but avoided the baroque excess that characterized too many of Detroit's offerings that year. **6.** Still, the previous simplicity of the side coves was meddled with, gaining strakes and dummy air scoops. Quad headlamps followed current trend, and the hood picked up simulated louvers. **7.** The back bumper now wrapped all the way to the rear wheel arches, and chrome stripes gussied up the deck.

Chevrolet cast an eye toward the lower-medium-priced segment of the market with its 1958 models. They were longer, wider, and bulkier looking. A new Impala sub-series pushed Chevy into higher-price territory and, in hardtop form, finally realized stylists' dreams of an "executive coupe."

The new A-body design featured gullwing rear fenders as an alternative to fins. Quad headlights and "thin-pillar" roof posts on sedans were new. Bob Veryzer, assistant chief designer, styled front parking-light housings inspired by jet-engine intakes.

6

1. The Corvette Impala, built for the 1956 Motorama, lent styling cues and its name to the '58 passenger-car line. 2-3. Two clay models of different scales and approaches to the 1958 Chevy photographed on November 21, 1955. 4-5. Another model from later that same month displayed a '57-like hood and front bumper, plus a divided backlight akin to what Buick and Olds would use. 6. This nonfunctional mock-up lacks the fuel-filler door that would have been set above the bumper. 7-8. The roof, taillights, and toothy grille of this December '55 model wouldn't last. 9. A comparison of mock-ups seen in September '56.

7

8

9

1. The 1958 Chevrolet convertible came only as an Impala. This two-car Bel Air subseries marked Chevy's entry into the lower end of the medium-priced market. All Impalas had stainless-steel rocker moldings and "pitchfork" trim ahead of the rear wheels. **2.** The now-four-door Nomad wagon was bigger and heavier than its predecessors, and had quad headlamps and parking lights. **3.** Twin-pod taillights and quieter trim identified the Bel Air four-door hardtop. **4.** Gullwing fins were graceful and subdued, at least for '58. The triple taillight clusters on this hardtop were an Impala exclusive.

3

There had never been a wilder-looking Chevrolet than the '59—and there probably hasn't been one to top it since. Swept up in the late-'56 frenzy to outfin future Chrysler products, Chevy made the switch to the corporate B-body with broad gullwing fins that tested manufacturing engineers' skills in bending sheetmetal.

Aside from the fins, the most memorable feature of the car was its "cat's-eye" taillamps, which were drawn up by Bob Cadaret. Headlamps sank into the ends of the grille for a lowered look.

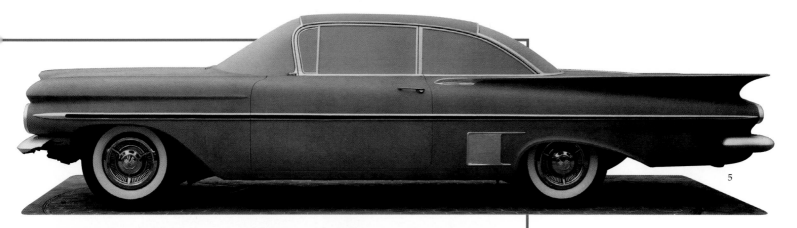

1-3. A Chuck Jordan rendering and two views of a small-scale clay model encapsulate the low, long motif for which Chevy was striving in its '59 cars. **4.** Already by January 11, 1957, Chevy stylists had lowered the headlamps to just above the bumper. The shallow elliptical detail in the center of the hood lost out to twin "nostrils" at the ends. **5-6.** In July '57, division chiefs were reviewing these hardtop proposals. The lower-body "vent" was dropped. **7.** Bizarre headlight arrangements were tried, then—wisely—rejected.

1

4

2

3

Once seen, never forgotten—that was the 1959 Chevy, mainly because of its perfectly outrageous cat's-eye taillights that glowered beneath bat-wing fins. A wildly wrapped four-door hardtop backlight and rear-roof overhang added to the effect. **1.** Impala became a full series that included this hardtop sedan. **2.** A Bel Air sedan displays the new grille "nostrils" and lowered headlights. **3.** A four-door hardtop shows why glass area increased a whopping 50 percent from 1958. **4-5.** An Impala convertible, with narrow side trim and a profoundly wrapped windshield.

5

1950 OLDSMOBILE

Oldsmobile, the oldest American make still in production at midcentury, began the 1950 styling cycle with new design leadership. Art Ross, who had penned the trend-setting "tombstone" grille for the 1941 Cadillac, succeeded George Snyder as studio head in early 1947.

The division entered the model year with three lines

1

2

3

1. A clay model of the 1950 Oldsmobile 98 on November 2, 1948. Its vertical A-pillar and wraparound windshield would finally reach production in the mid Fifties. **2.** In the end, the bumper/grille and hood sculpting would be dialed back. **3.** High, round taillights became an Olds style mark. **4.** "Hockey stick" side trim was another touch that would be used later.

of cars. The six-cylinder 76 and lively V-8-equipped 88 were on the year-old A-body, and got a token detail facelift. The premium 98 shifted to the new B-body, where it was offered in five body styles, including two- and four-door fastbacks.

Despite the change in administration, there was a stylistic continuity. Ross retained the frowning "fishmouth" grille theme Snyder had developed for Oldses of the late Forties.

4

5

6

5. Hardtop styling, an innovation first seen on 1949 GM C-body cars, was extended to A-body cars like this "Futuramic" Olds 88 for 1950. The car ran with a hardy 303.7-cid "Rocket" V-8. Chrome fins that held the taillights and reshaped stone shields were changes from 1949. **6.** This 98 four-door sedan shows the integrated rear-fender look ushered in with the new B-body for 1950.

Nineteen fifty-three proved to be the last go-round for the look pioneered by the 98 of 1950. Small detail and side-trim changes had taken place in the interim. (Four-door sedans also got a reshaped backlight and C-pillar.) A Super 88 series arrived for 1951 on the OB-body shared with the Buick Special; the base Deluxe 88 adopted these shells in '52.

For 1953, Oldsmobile cribbed Cadillac's canted front-bumper guards, but topped them in elliptical pods. All 88s got tall rear quarters. The limited-edition Fiesta came with a dipped beltline and wrapped windshield.

1. A major revision of the Olds bumper/grille for 1952 or '53 was proposed, as this March 1950 photo reveals. Relocation of parking lights was also eyed. **2.** In June '50, the grille on this clay (with 1952-style 98 side trim) went without ribs. **3.** Fendertop scoops, possibly for ventilation, were tried in April 1950.

4

5

4. Elliptical pods atop the canted bumper guards, as on this '53 Super 88 Holiday, would become a familiar Olds shape during the next few years, showing up on grilles and taillights. **5.** The limited-production Ninety-Eight Fiesta convertible sported "dream car" touches that included a wrapped windshield and dipped beltline. The horizontal grille divider was now more pronounced. **6.** A Ninety-Eight Holiday shows the division's signature bullet taillights.

6

1

Did they, or didn't they? That's the question that underlies Oldsmobile's new look for 1954.

Division General Manager Jack Wolfram told the press that the '54s had been intended as the 1955 models. There's some doubt that General Motors could have sped up schedules that quickly, especially since Buick—which shared the B-body Olds used— would have been involved, too. However, some auto historians believe Wolfram's statement.

2

3

1. A facelifted early Fifties B-body with grille, bumper, hood, and parking-light details akin to what would be used on the rebodied '54s. The car also has a new low-profile cowl-ventilator panel. By some accounts, GM executive Harlow Curtice didn't like the warmed-over appearance, which touched off an effort to get a new look for 1954. **2-3.** This incomplete clay for the Ninety-Eight sedan from March 10, 1953, wears trim ultimately reserved for the hardtop and convertible. **4.** Teardrop rear wheel arches were picked for the sportier '54 Ninety-Eight models.

4

5

6

7

8

Oldsmobiles were redesigned for 1954. Although the evolution was a natural one, it was also dramatic. **5-6.** A '54 Ninety-Eight Holiday hardtop coupe showing asymmetrical side trim and a hood that's lower relative to the fendertops than before. Swept-back wheel arches imparted a sense of motion. Bullet taillamps were continued, and the rear side trim culminated in the back-up lights. **7.** The "Panoramic" windshield was built-in to all models, like this Super 88 hardtop. **8.** A Super 88 convertible shows off the new thinner bright trim for the upper grille.

Perhaps the most striking appearance change to the facelifted 1955 and '56 Oldsmobiles was a shift from the Forties-vintage "frowning" grille. Art Ross's studio turned out several Motorama show cars with elliptical grilles, starting with the '53 Starfire convertible. The '55 production cars adopted this shape, filling the cavity with the expected twin pods. The following year saw a move to horizontal bars and a vertical center divider.

Swept-back front wheelwells, a feature exclusive to Ninety-Eights in '54, were extended linewide in '55. All series added hooded headlights, too.

4

5

6

1. Its new face essentially complete, this February 9, 1954, mock-up of the '55 Ninety-Eight sedan still needed to have its side trim resolved before the start of production. **2-3.** One big grille bar or many small ones for '56? The topic was open for discussion in July '54. **4.** Though Olds hadn't offered a station wagon since 1950, this odd two-door model was being modeled in May 1954. **5-6.** The brightwork on this '56 Ninety-Eight model (5) was near final; the Dodge-like trim on the 88 (6) was not. **7-8.** The 1955 Ninety-Eight line included a convertible and all-new hardtop sedan. **9-10.** Super 88 two- and four-door hardtops from 1956.

9

10

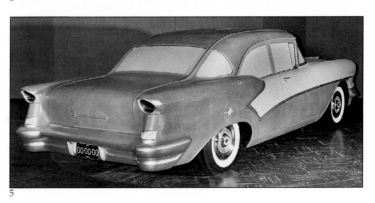

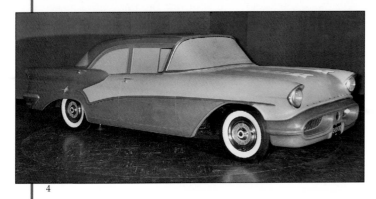

The styling of the 1957 Oldsmobiles was subject to the same forces at work in the rest of Harley Earl's General Motors styling studios. The overall lowering of hoods and roofs was offset by a puffing out of body panels and a bulking up of marque-specific design cues.

Taillights still rode high, but they went from being round "bullets" to flat ovals at the end of tubular booms atop the rear quarters. "Hockey stick" side trim came back—wider and with paint-filled centers. A broader version of the '56 grille served up front. Station wagons, including a hardtop, returned.

1-3. In May 1955, bumpers, taillights, and trim for 1957 were far from settled. The B-body cars shared roofs with Buick. **4-5.** Two months later, 88 brightwork was still up for grabs, but taillamp and rear bumper designs were rounding into shape. **6-7.** A Ninety-Eight clay from July 1955 almost has the '57 trim down pat. Trunklid detailing would be simpler, though. **8.** Rocket hood ornaments were added by September. **9.** A wagon mock-up with fixed-post and pillarless sides. **10.** The still-unfinished grille, April 6, 1956.

6

7

8

9

10

1. Olds was noticeably lower for '57, and a bit longer, too. This is a Ninety-Eight Starfire coupe. **2-3.** A Holiday hardtop and a convertible—both Super 88s—show the year's massive bumper wrap and undivided grille. Rear-quarter trim that began at the front doors with an intriguing curve culminated in a rigid horizontal element. Concurrent Buicks, with which Olds shared bodies, had a livelier treatment. **4.** Wagon buyers could go in style with the Super 88 Fiesta hardtop. The modest wrap of the backlight was pleasing, but chrome was creeping onto the taillight surrounds. Made in hardtop and fixed-pillar styles, these were the first Oldsmobile wagons since 1950.

3

1   2

General Motors's loss of momentum as the U.S. auto industry's style leader was apparent in its 1958 models. Exhibit A was that year's line of Oldsmobiles.

Viewed from the front, fenders billowed up over the new quad headlights. The hood appeared to be pumped up—and out—as well, as if the optional air suspension had suddenly sprung a leak and inflated the whole car with escaping vapor. Apart from round taillights, Olds styling cues of recent years were gone. Massive front-bumper pods appeared to be anchoring the car in place. The L-shaped rear-quarter trim was replaced by a stack of chrome spears.

5

1-2. In the early months of 1956, Oldsmobile stylists were pursuing an update of the relatively restrained '57 design that would have incorporated a modified bumper/grille and four headlights. 3-4. By July 31, however, the direction had swung drastically toward a far "busier" look. The high-riding taillights of years past were almost replaced by chrome "bullets." By this time the pointed pods that encompassed the headlights were sculpted into the bodysides. Also of note, the three-piece backlight design used on the '57s was already out the window—pardon the pun. 5-6. The '58 Olds design was virtually complete by November 29, 1956. The lower-body spear was an element that had been considered for many GM designs throughout the Fifties.

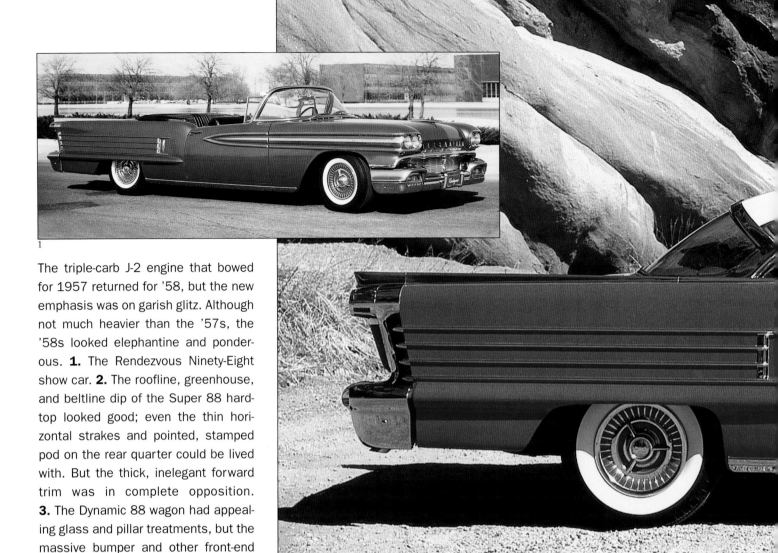

1

The triple-carb J-2 engine that bowed for 1957 returned for '58, but the new emphasis was on garish glitz. Although not much heavier than the '57s, the '58s looked elephantine and ponderous. **1.** The Rendezvous Ninety-Eight show car. **2.** The roofline, greenhouse, and beltline dip of the Super 88 hardtop looked good; even the thin horizontal strakes and pointed, stamped pod on the rear quarter could be lived with. But the thick, inelegant forward trim was in complete opposition. **3.** The Dynamic 88 wagon had appealing glass and pillar treatments, but the massive bumper and other front-end glitter were out of control. **4.** At the rear, as on this Super 88 ragtop, GM's aviation motif became self-parody.

2

3

Oldsmobile dubbed the thoroughly new styling of its 1959 cars "The Linear Look." Born of the hurried corporate scramble to change design directions, it was cleaner and simpler than the styling it replaced.

The '59 Olds design effort began under Art Ross, but was finished by Irv Rybicki, who succeeded him as studio head in May 1957. It was Rybicki who, with input from a friend, Pontiac's Jack Humbert, came up with the dropped-center hood and "barbell" grille that made it onto the production design.

The long taillight-boom design originated when Harley Earl saw a big rocket model Ross had brought to the studio, and had someone hold it up to the side of a clay model in progress. Staff stylist Ed Taylor devised the oval taillights.

1. A six-window four-door hardtop clay from March 19, 1957. The six-window hardtop ultimately would be denied to Oldsmobile. **2.** The Olds side of the station wagon model also seen on page 167. **3.** The horizontal bars proposed in this October 1, 1957, full-size rear rendering for the Ninety-Eight weren't used. **4-5.** Like the other GM makes, Olds dabbled in unorthodox headlight arrangements. Triple taillight clusters were under consideration, too. **6-7.** The low fin in picture 6 and the side trim in picture 7 were close to the accepted styles.

4

5

6

7

1

2

248

Olds began to regain its design footing for '59. **1.** Although side trim, as on this Ninety-Eight convertible, was mercifully restrained, the widely spaced headlights were somewhat odd. **2.** Elliptical elements returned, this time as taillights. On Ninety-Eights, like this hardtop sedan, they were curved. Knife-edged fins had a subtle rise, and looked smart and slippery; fin/taillight chromework no longer shouted. **3.** A longer, lower stance, seen here on a Ninety-Eight "SceniCoupe," erased the tanklike look of the previous year. **4-5.** The Dynamic 88 two-door sedan (4) and Ninety-Eight Celebrity four-door sedan (5). Olds easily adapted the Buick door design in GM's body-sharing plan.

3

4

5

Pontiac's plan for changing the looks of its cars in the early Fifties would have been right at home 30 or 40 years later. The 1951 and '52 models were retrimmed body doubles of the 1949-50 cars, Pontiac's first completely new postwar models designed under the direction of Robert Lauer.

Distinct Pontiac touches like round taillights (in use since 1948) and central bands of "Silver Streak" trim (in use since 1935) continued, but detail changes were made. New side trim and a "V"-center grille came in for 1951. Bodyside decoration was changed again for '52, and the top bar of the grille was altered.

6

7

9

8

1-4. Fastback sedan proposals from August 9, 1949, imagine a '51 Pontiac built on the Buick/Oldsmobile OB-body. The 1951-52 Pontiacs continued on the corporate A-body. **5.** A drawing from April '46 for a new steel-bodied station wagon. Pontiac built wagons to this basic design from 1949 to 1952, but only with four doors. **6-7.** A "gullwing" grille and spearpoint side trim on DeLuxe models identified the '51s. **8-9.** A dummy scoop atop the grille and new wheel covers came for '52.

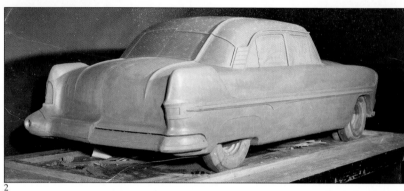

For 1953, Pontiac had a substantially new look that was created under new leadership. Raoul Pepin succeeded Bob Lauer as chief designer in the Pontiac Studio in 1951. Pepin's staff had to use an updated version of the 1949-52 A-body, but was granted a two-inch gain in wheelbase around which to create a design.

As might be expected, there was a new grille, plus somewhat Packard-like side trim on DeLuxes. Bright stone shields on the premium-level cars curved in concert with the separate-looking rear fenders, running all the way back to the bumpers to accentuate the sense of length. The ends of the rear fenders rose in squared-off blades, a touch that would appear on Pontiacs through '56.

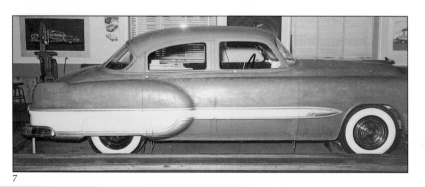

1-4. Even as they completed the production design for 1953, Pontiac stylists were looking ahead to subsequent years. These small-scale clay models from August 29 (1, 2) and October 11, 1951 (3, 4), hinted at what was to come. **5-6.** Grille and DeLuxe/standard trim styles were nearly final on this December 7, 1950, model, but the fastback body wouldn't last into '53. **7.** A rejected side-trim plan from April '51.

1

2

Although the '53 Pontiacs still had bodyside bulges that suggested separate rear fenders, windshields and backlights now were single pieces. The 122-inch wheelbase was two inches longer than before, allowing for a seemingly massive design that was in keeping with buyer preference. **1.** The "Silver Streak" theme was elaborated upon, and now was called "Dual Streak"; the trim is seen here on a Custom Catalina. This touch, and the squared-off fins, would define the marque visually for the next several years. **2.** The emphatic hood ornament, add-on sun visor, and chrome stone shields that extended along the skirts to the back bumper made the Chieftain Eight Catalina hardtop a looker. Indian-head badging at the fins reiterated the Pontiac trademark. **3.** The vertical taillights used on Chieftain station wagons were reworked units from the '53 Chevy, with which Pontiac shared bodies. This six-seat Eight DeLuxe was one of 12 Pontiac wagons for '53.

1955-56 PONTIAC

Like Chevrolet, with which it shared bodies, Pontiac was attempting to create a lively new V-8-powered image for itself in 1955. This was signaled on the outside by fresh styling and some exciting new models.

Early in 1953, Paul Gillan became chief designer, in time to direct work on the '55s. It was he who styled the car's distinctive bumper/grille unit. Small faux vents sat atop the front fenders, slightly behind the projected headlights. The flat hood featured parallel Silver Streaks and a small scoop at the bottom, touches taken from the '53 Parisienne show car. An idea attributed to Homer LaGassey was the flattening of the edges of the rear fenders and covering them with Silver Streaks of their own.

The Safari, Pontiac's take on the Chevy Nomad wagon, arrived for 1955. Four-door hardtops were added in 1956, the year a "chromier" grille was adopted.

1. The '55 Strato-Star dream car showed off the new headlight design and presaged the '56 bumper. **2.** The 1955 bumper/grille was well defined by July 27, 1953, but headlights and hood trim would be revised. **3.** At one point, a grille mesh cribbed from the Strato-Star was considered for the 1956 update. **4-5.** However, in mid 1954, Pontiac stylists had already come up with bumper/grille ideas closer to what would be produced for '56.

1-2. Pontiac hoods now were flat rather than humped, and the decorative Dual Streaks were more widely separated than in 1954. Newly recessed headlamps were topped by gimmicky, scooplike hoods. Grilles acquired a hunkier, more sculpted look, and more emphatic verticals stamped into the "upper lip." Some observers felt the cars had a flat-nose look. These are '55 Star Chief convertibles. **3.** Although rooflines were shared with Chevy, Pontiac had its own character, as a glance at this 1955 Star Chief two-door

hardtop makes clear. The optional hood ornament now had a larger amber segment, and three body-side stars signaled it was a Star Chief. **4.** Pontiac sheetmetal was unchanged for '56, but grilles picked up additional chrome. Round parking lights flanked rocket-pod doodads, and the Star Chief "stars" were replaced with flattened ovals at the rear quarters. **5.** The bed of the 1956 Safari had carpeting and chrome skid strips. Taillights were hooded linewide. **6.** Bodyside two-toning was revised for '56, as on this Star Chief four-door hardtop.

4

5

6

1 9 5 7   P O N T I A C

The design of the 1957 Pontiac is as famous for what *wasn't* on it as for what was. When Semon E. "Bunkie" Knudsen took over as divisional general manager on July 1, 1956, he decided he'd seen enough of Silver Streaks. He ordered them removed from the '57s, then just weeks from entering production—and never mind that it had been his father, William, who had approved

1

2

them for Pontiacs in the first place in the Thirties.

A second facelift of the '55 A-body, the 1957 featured hooded headlights, pointed rear fenders, and a waterfall grille drawn by Irv Rybicki. The new limited-edition Bonneville convertible was trimmed to emphasize its fuel-injected power.

3

1. The round taillights of recent Pontiacs became elliptical for '57. Chevy-like fins were in evidence in April 1955. 2. Stylists eventually went for angled fenders with a diecast insert. 3. As of July 1955, a slotted version of the eventual grille style was in place on this mock-up. 4. By February '56, the design still did not have the rocket-silhouette side trim that would become Pontiac's temporary identifier. 5. March 8, 1956: Silver Streaks on borrowed time. 6. A fiberglass mock-up of Bonneville trim in August 1956.

1

2

4

Although still based on the corporate A-body, the '57 Pontiacs had a fresh look and a new model. **1.** The convertible-only Bonneville was named after the Utah salt flats where speed records were set. All Pontiacs had 347-cid V-8s, but Bonnevilles ran with fuel injection, and had exclusive gravel shields, hash-mark trim, spinner wheel covers, and unique side trim. **2.** Safari showed the new side-cove treatment, elevated fins, and elliptical taillamps. **3.** Chieftain wagons were more subdued. **4-5.** Chieftain two- and four-door sedans; the "waterfall" grille was new.

3

5

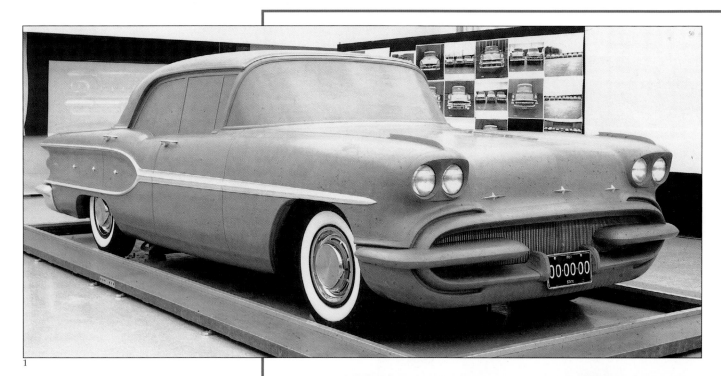

In the absence of the Silver Streaks and images of Chief Pontiac, cues that had signaled "Pontiac" to passersby for years, the division needed something to identify its cars. For the time being, Pontiac would recycle 1957's rocket side-trim motif for its all-new A-body '58s—even if it was redolent with Olds imagery.

No model embraced the rocket theme to the extent the Bonneville did. Aside from the convertible, there was now a two-door hard-top in the Chevy Impala mold. Concave flanks, quad headlights *and* taillights, and a mesh grille were part of the look for all '58s.

1-2. By February 17, 1956, the '58 design included a grille that adapted the '55 theme and the beginnings of a move toward quad taillights. The 1956-57 hardtop sedan roof wouldn't last, and the forward portion of the side trim would be opened up. **3.** Just days earlier, the clay model had incorporated high wedge-shaped taillights and bumper exhaust outlets. **4.** The emerging Bonneville hardtop design on August 24, 1956. The delta-shaped side trim would survive on Star Chiefs. **5.** A 1958 fiberglass mock-up compared to the '57 production design on September 7, 1956. Decklid grooves would be reserved for Bonnevilles and Chieftain convertibles. **6.** The rocket-fin cove trim and angled hash marks on this Star Chief model would shift to Bonnevilles. **7.** On November 9, 1956, this station wagon clay was in progress. Note the hardtop styling—and 1957 Chevy wheel covers.

1

2

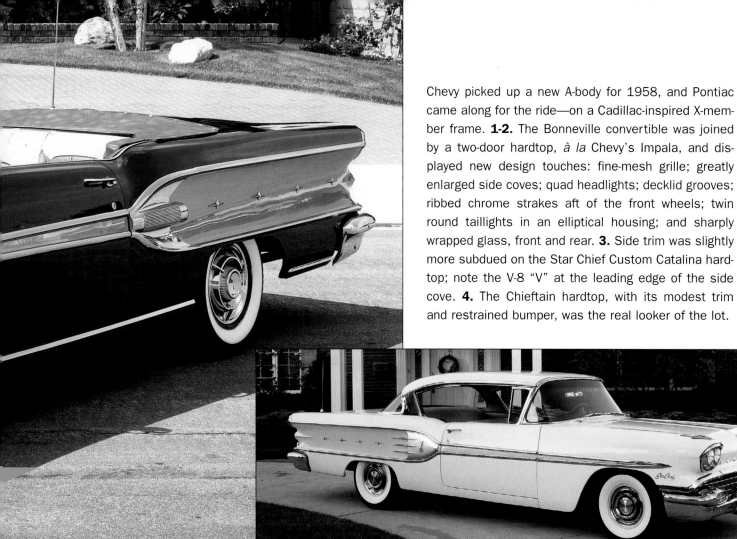

Chevy picked up a new A-body for 1958, and Pontiac came along for the ride—on a Cadillac-inspired X-member frame. **1-2.** The Bonneville convertible was joined by a two-door hardtop, *à la* Chevy's Impala, and displayed new design touches: fine-mesh grille; greatly enlarged side coves; quad headlights; decklid grooves; ribbed chrome strakes aft of the front wheels; twin round taillights in an elliptical housing; and sharply wrapped glass, front and rear. **3.** Side trim was slightly more subdued on the Star Chief Custom Catalina hardtop; note the V-8 "V" at the leading edge of the side cove. **4.** The Chieftain hardtop, with its modest trim and restrained bumper, was the real looker of the lot.

3

4

1959 PONTIAC

By the time the Pontiac Studio was finished with its 1959 design, it had created a car that quite literally was new from top to bottom. Not only did it have a strikingly low and long body, but its widely spaced wheels—an idea developed by Chuck Jordan in a special-projects studio—gave it an aggressive stance. Pontiac called it "Wide Track."

Once Pontiac stylists threw out the '58-based designs on which they'd started, they came up with arguably the most striking bodies in GM's 1959 fleet. As early as April '56, Carl Renner had sketched something akin to the production car's oblong taillights and bladelike bumper ends while working in an advanced-design studio. Several months before he was transferred out of the Pontiac Studio, Paul Gillan drew the split grille that, like Wide Track, would be a Pontiac trademark for years.

1

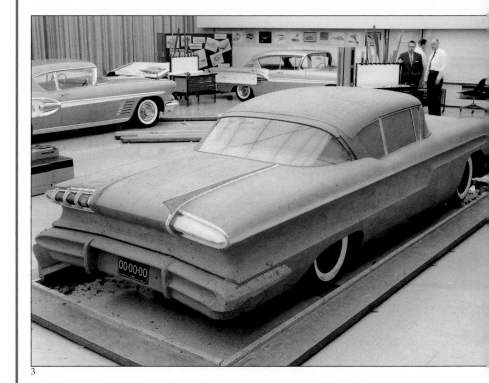

3

4

5

1-3. The earliest '59 Pontiac design, seen in January 1957, played off the rounded 1958 themes. Studio chief Paul Gillan (picture 3, in suit) reviews the progress. **4-5.** A crash redesign program produced this Chrysler-like car with blade fins (designers called them "bunny ears") by May '57. **6-8.** The accepted look included small "V" fins and a twin-element grille. Gillan's June 26, 1957, sketch (7) set the tone.

1

2

3

A five-inch increase in front track width (to 63.7) and nearly as much at the rear meant that "Wide-Track" Pontiacs had arrived. **1-2.** As with other GM lines, Pontiac was considerably less baroque for '59: New split grilles were simple, bumpers less ornamental, and side trim was more muted than before; the previous side coves were only hinted at. Even the V-capped fins were relatively modest. These are the Bonneville hardtop coupe and convertible. **3-4.** Bonneville offered two new models for '59; a Safari wagon and the Vista hardtop sedan. Note the great glass area and slim pillars.

4

KAISER-FRAZER CORPORATION

In its brief existence, Kaiser-Frazer managed to have more than its share of design successes, aided by the fact that both Henry Kaiser and Joseph Frazer keenly appreciated the role styling played in selling automobiles. They were fortunate to have a virtual all-star team of stylists—some on the company payroll, some as consultants—working for them at one time or another, including Howard "Dutch" Darrin, Brooks Stevens, Bob Cadwallader, Cliff Voss, Herb Weissinger, Buzz Grisinger, John Chika, Damon Woods, Duncan McRae, Bob Robillard, and Alex Tremulis.

Known for his svelte prewar Packard Darrin convertibles and the first Packard Clipper with its blended-fender bodyside, Dutch Darrin was hired by Joe Frazer, then head of Graham-Paige, to design that company's postwar automobile. Announced late in 1945 and put into production as a '47 model, the Frazer was America's first slab-sided, envelope-body car.

Darrin himself was not totally pleased with the design. For one thing, what he regarded as preliminary, G-P engineers took as finished work. For another, in developing the Frazer, the engineers eliminated the "Darrin dip" in the rear door, which Dutch regarded as his trademark. He was so displeased that he demanded a "Styled by Darrin" script be removed from the cars' decklids, even though such public credit to a designer was an honor unprecedented on a production automobile.

In August 1945, seeking additional capital, Joe Frazer teamed up with Henry Kaiser, a West Coast magnate who dreamed of entering the automobile business. Though Henry had some ambitious ideas, including front-wheel drive and torsion-bar suspension, the '47 Kaiser wound up as a conventional, less-expensive Frazer.

The basic K-F four-door body remained in production into 1950. However, the design was refreshed by variants like Kaiser Virginians and Frazer Manhattans, and a combination sedan/wagon, the hatchback Traveler/Vagabond.

In spring 1950, Kaiser-Frazer introduced its 1951 models. The most clever was the Frazer, which continued to use the 1947 body but with new fronts and rears. Again Darrin was frustrated, wanting to introduce his "dip" into the design, but getting stuck with carryover doors. Even so, the '51 Frazer was a smart-looking turnout. So successful was the facelift that few knew (or cared) that the shell was carried over. Created primarily to use up leftover bodies, Frazer production ended when its body supply dried up.

A much bigger disappointment to Darrin was K-F's new small car named after Henry J. Kaiser, who wanted to fulfill his ambition of building a low-priced car "for the masses." Based on a design created at American Metal Products, the Henry J had the same 100-inch wheelbase as the Nash Rambler, but the resemblance stopped there. The Henry J car was a strange duck, combining Frazer and Kaiser styling cues, while the first year's cars lacked such expected amenities as a glovebox and decklid. The Henry J never recovered from its initial perception as a "cheap car," and when the Kaisers took over Willys-Overland, the Henry J was jettisoned in favor of the Aero-Willys.

In the 1951 Kaiser, however, Darrin finally achieved what he was seeking. At its introduction, the car was arguably the best-looking sedan in America, and it was replete with Darrin touches: the famed "dip" highlighting the rear quarters, the "sweetheart" windshield, and the distinctive high-arched side glass. Chrome was carried low on the body, and the grille opening was fronted by a simple bright bar. During the next two model years, the grille bar got heavier and the taillights bigger, yet the design remained attractive. Exterior color selection and interior design were the work of Carleton Spencer, K-F's color wizard, who was also responsible for the glamorous Dragons, and the "Bambu" vinyl and exotic fabrics of Kaiser interiors.

In 1954, the front end was changed to accept a concave grille inspired by the Buick XP-300 concept car (precluding Buick from using its own design). "Safety-Glo" taillights and a wraparound rear window altered the look out back. But what the car really needed was a V-8, an undertaking then beyond K-F's financial abilities. Due to the turmoil of moving production from Willow Run, Michigan, to Toledo, Ohio, the 1954 model year got off to a slow start from which the Kaiser never recovered. A token number of '55s were run off, most going to Argentina as the Kaisers ended automobile production in the United States.

Darrin's other Kaiser was the fiberglass-bodied Kaiser-Darrin sports car, built in its own plant in Jackson, Michigan. From the side or rear, the two-seater was decent looking, its chief design innovation being sliding doors that disappeared into the front fenders. The front end was, to say the least, unusual, featuring a petite, puckered-up grille that, in addition to looking odd, didn't appear large enough to cool the Willys engine underhood. Nevertheless, the 1954 Kaiser-Darrin remains highly collectible.

Though it was originally intended to be a post-World War II revival of the moribund Graham, the car named for veteran auto-industry executive Joseph Frazer got a new identity soon after he joined forces with Henry J. Kaiser in 1945. Kaiser-Frazer Corporation's upper-medium-priced make only lasted a mere five model years, but it attracted a surprising number of talented designers in that brief span.

Howard "Dutch" Darrin, celebrated for his custom-body designs in the interwar years, came up with the slab-sided look of the original '47 Frazer. He disavowed it, though, when the production car came out sans his cherished "Darrin dip" in the unbroken fenderline. For 1949-50, former Chrysler stylist Herb Weissinger updated the design with a taller eggcrate grille and vertical taillights.

Weissinger fashioned a more-drastic facelift for the final Kaiser of 1951. He even incorporated a version of the Darrin dip, albeit too far back to please Dutch.

1

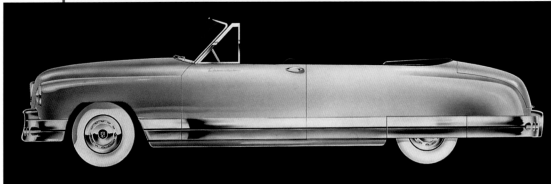

2

5

Noted industrial designer Brooks Stevens was hired to provide Frazer styling ideas. **1-2.** Drawings dated March 24, 1948, show his ideas for a prospective 1950 sedan with a low-mouth bumper/grille, and a convertible coupe. **3.** Another sedan proposal from October '48. **4.** Yet another take on the low-grille theme. **5-7.** Stevens also drew up dramatic interior concepts.

Frazers were clean-lined cars powered by an industrial Continental six that adapted poorly to road use. **1.** Early Frazers were styled by engineers John Maxwell and Conrad Rehbein, working from a scale model by Dutch Darrin. Darrin disliked the results, though his very modern integral fenderline was retained, as on this '49 Manhattan ragtop. **2.** The 1951 Manhattan hardtop had a distinctive, if heavy, grille, and an approximation of the "Darrin dip" in the fenderline. **3.** Vagabond utility sedans appeared for '51, even though Joe Frazer had not wanted them for his uplevel nameplate. Note the fendertop taillights.

1

2

3

Before he was in the car business, Henry J. Kaiser wanted to build a small, inexpensive automobile. After he got his hands on a car company of his own in the late Forties, he was determined to do it.

Kaiser became enamored of a stubby fastback design

pitched to him by a wealthy Detroit investor. Dutch Darrin begged company officials to build a scaled-down version of his '51 Kaiser design for the new small car, and Duncan McRae of the in-house styling group came up with another concept. Both were rejected. (Darrin wound up helping with the production design; McRae quit the company.)

For a 1952 facelift, Herb Weissinger used a Frazer-inspired grille. Taillights moved into the fins, which deliberately aped Cadillac.

1. In-house designer Duncan McRae proposed this 100-inch-wheelbase sedan. 2. Consultant Dutch Darrin pushed this small-car design derived from his work on the '51 Kaiser. 3. The frameless door glass in this illustration turned up on an early Henry J prototype. 4. Possible variations to the fastback sedan body—such as this convertible—were drawn up from time to time. 5-9. Proposed grille and taillight styles for the 1952 facelift. 10. This Herb Weissinger idea for a grille found its way onto Henry Js sold from mid 1952 through 1954.

1

2

1. During its brief life, the Henry J was offered as a two-door fastback sedan only. Although the design was handsome, the fastback configuration had fallen out of favor with buyers and manufacturers. Notable features, as seen on this 1951 Six, include a simple but emphatic grille, slantback front fenders, stamped bodyside creases, and subdued tailfins. By this time, though, divided windshields were becoming passé. The J's basic configuration was the work of American Metal Products (AMP). 2. The appeal of chromeless side accents is evident on this '51. Note the contoured wheel-arch lips. 3. Dutch Darrin's early studies for a small Kaiser were rejected, but he was later brought on board to tweak AMP's Henry J concept. Darrin added his "dip" just aft of the door, and did side and rear windows that recalled the big Kaiser. 4-5. A '53 Corsair with a cleaner grille, vertical Cadillac-like taillamps, and back-up lights.

1

When word got out that Kaiser was planning a redesign for 1951, Dutch Darrin—who still had a contract with K-F—put his hat in the ring. Consultant Brooks Stevens and the in-house staff headed by Arnott "Buzz" Grisinger would also submit ideas. Darrin's low beltline, sloping roof, and raked windshield carried the day with Henry Kaiser. Even Grisinger conceded it was "the right choice."

2

3

4

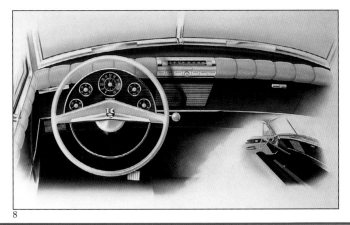

5

1. In May 1950, the head of the Kaiser styling studio, Buzz Grisinger, drew this proposal for a convertible off Dutch Darrin's '51 Kaiser design. **2.** Before Darrin got involved, others were already working to replace the first-series Kaiser design. Consultant Brooks Stevens presented this concept in December '47. **3.** This Stevens rendering from July 1948 offers a bit more flair. **4-7.** A range of possible body variations from Stevens is dated December 9, 1948. **8-9.** As he had done for Frazer, Stevens presented interior ideas using a centrally mounted instrument cluster.

6

7

8

9

1

The early postwar years were good ones for Kaiser-Frazer, but by 1949 competition from the Big Three—particularly Ford and GM—was fierce. Kaiser designers Dutch Darrin, Duncan McRae, Herb Weissinger, Alex Tremulis, and Buzz Grisinger rose to the challenge. **1.** Sleek and sure-footed, the '51s still ran with the adapted industrial engine once used to power forklifts. This Traveler Deluxe two-door shows its graceful grille and dipped "sweetheart" windshield. **2.** Salesmen made effective use of the Traveler, seen here in four-door form. **3.** The rake of the Kaiser windshield was the industry's steepest in 1951; the elegant roofline and side-window treatment show the Darrin touch. This is a Dragon, which came in an array of color schemes and fabrics that were the brainchild of K-F color stylist Carleton Spencer. Imaginative two-toning was enhanced by complementary interior hues. The combo seen here, with black vinyl over Arena Yellow (and black vinyl interior), was dubbed the "Golden Dragon." Other Dragons were "Silver," "Emerald," and "Jade." **4.** The '51 Kaiser had the lowest beltline and greatest glass area, industrywide. This Special two-door sedan has the signature dipped backlight.

2

3

4

Former Chrysler stylist Buzz Grisinger came to Kaiser-Frazer in 1947 to work on advanced designs, but soon was put in charge of Kaiser styling. After freshening up Dutch Darrin's '51 Kaiser design for 1952-53, Grisinger was chiefly responsible for a more ambitious facelift scheduled for the 1954 car.

The front of Grisinger's '54 Kaiser borrowed liberally from the '51 Buick XP-300 show car, especially in the grille and headlamp bezels. It featured a wraparound rear window and large "Safety-Glo" taillights.

Darrin's presence still was felt at K-F in this period. He sold Henry Kaiser on the idea of bringing out a two-seat sports car for '54, the fiberglass-bodied Kaiser-Darrin.

4

5

1. Styling studio head Arnott "Buzz" Grisinger with a mock-up of his facelift for the 1954 Kaiser, circa 1951. The concave grille and oval headlamp housings were copied from the Buick XP-300 show car that company president Edgar Kaiser admired. Grisinger added a hood scoop and bold canted bumper guards. Cost issues toned down the latter, though. **2-8.** Grisinger soon went out on his own, but still provided ideas to Kaiser. Bob Gurr, a young designer who had recently quit Ford, was recruited to come up with more sketches for Grisinger for possible updates.

6

7

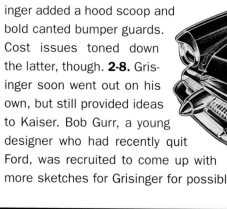

8

Kaiser design chief Buzz Grisinger supervised a clever, stunningly good-looking makeover for 1954. **1-2.** A low beltline and generous glass, as on this Manhattan four-door sedan, continued. The oval headlight housings and concave, vertical-stripe grille were suggested by Edgar Kaiser, who had liked the ideas when he saw them on Buick's earlier XP-300 show car. The Manhattan had a dramatically wrapped backlight and boasted beautifully shaped "Safety-Glo" taillamps with fendertop extensions. Bumper guards were canted, and a hood scoop replaced the mascot. A McCulloch centrifugal turbo boosted horsepower from 118 to 140, and inside, passenger crash padding was added, front and rear. **3.** The entry-level '54 was the handsome Special. Early versions lacked the wraparound backlight.

1

1. Because the '54 redesign ate up dwindling Kaiser resources, the main visual change to the '55 Manhattan—by now Kaiser's sole model—was a taller fin atop the hood scoop. **2-3.** In 1952, designer Dutch Darrin spent his own money to design a sports car of glass-reinforced plastic to ride the Henry J chassis. Introduced as a '54 model, the Kaiser-Darrin (so named by Henry Kaiser) had a three-way folding top with an available fiberglass hard-top, a medallionlike grille piece above a concave nose section, a long hood, tapering rear quarters, and teardrop taillights adapted from standard '52 Kaiser units. A handful were super-charged. Considerable interest was generated by the doors, which slid forward electrically on rollers. They didn't slide forward quite far enough, though, making entry and exit a chore. Before the flaw could be addressed, production of the rakish Kaiser-Darrin was suspended after only 435 units.

2

3

PACKARD MOTOR CAR COMPANY

Packard entered the Fifties in search of an identity. This is, of course, ironic, given that it had benefited from one of the industry's most enduring styling trademarks for nearly half a century. The familiar vertical radiator grille with its yoke-shaped pinnacle had graced the front of every Packard since 1904—and the estate driveways of America's most socially prominent and wealthiest families. But in the upbeat, in-with-the-new America of the Fifties, vertical grilles were as old hat as running boards.

Had Packard been a European marque, this would not have been a problem. Mercedes-Benz, Rolls-Royce, Bentley, Jaguar, Daimler, and other luxury marques were able to continue using time-honored vertical-grille motifs without looking obsolete. But in this country, continued use of an upright grille was impossible, yet Packard had no other styling uniqueness. Dutch Darrin's distinctive, graceful fadeaway fenders of the prewar Clipper had been plastered over to create the "bathtub" Packard of 1948-50 (which, to be fair, was better thought of at the time than it is now). When John Reinhart's all-new Packard arrived for 1951, the stylists attempted to retain traces of the traditional Packard identity in the yoke shape of the grille opening and the concave scallops in the hood. Somehow, it just

wasn't enough. What's more, while light years ahead of the amorphous "bathtub," Packards through 1954 were rather plain and inexpensive looking, with important style elements ill-conceived. For example, there weren't any front-to-back side-molding treatments until 1953, and the senior two-door hardtop and convertible had to make do with the junior series quarter panels and taillights. While archrival Cadillac was creating distinctive marque-identifying cues front, side, and rear, Packard struggled to find itself.

Enter James Nance. Say what you will about Nance, the former General Electric/Hotpoint executive knew what had to be done to lift Packard out of the doldrums. In resurrecting the Clipper name in 1953, he sought to put distance between the junior and senior Packards. He commissioned specialty body constructor Henney (with its in-house stylist, Richard Arbib) to create the comely Pan American show car, then commissioned Mitchell-Bentley Corporation to build a production version, naming it Caribbean. Working with Henney, Nance revived limousines and eight-passenger sedans, then added a standard-wheelbase padded-roof sedan by Derham, another old-line custom coachbuilder. But the all-new Packard Nance really wanted had to wait until 1955.

Though it added a modern V-8 and industry-leading torsion-bar suspension, the 1955-56 Packard had to make do with carryover bodies cleverly facelifted by the talented Dick Teague. What's not usually understood is that Teague's Packards were replete with Cadillac styling cues, including "Dagmar" bumper bombs, eggcrate grillework, a simulated air intake on the rear quarters, exaggerated taillights, wraparound windshield, and ornamental "V"s scattered everywhere.

Still searching for a modern Packard identity (and in answer to many customer letters), Teague grafted an upright grille onto a Packard Four Hundred hardtop and named the concept vehicle "Request." But this attempted morphing of old and new wasn't the answer. What *should* have been the answer was the wildly futuristic-looking Predictor show car. Fronting this ultramodern hardtop was a tall, slim interpretation of the traditional Packard grille shape, this time functioning not as a grille but as an oversized vertical bumper guard.

Nance had been busy building an impressive styling team, led by vice president William Schmidt, the Lincoln Futura designer lured away from Ford. Separate studios were set up for the senior cars, Clipper, and Packard's new dance partner, Studebaker. A Predictor-themed Packard line and equally new Clippers and Studebakers—all with shared inner-body panels—were slated for 1957, then for 1958. . . .

The stumbling block was that Nance's

1954 merger with Studebaker had not been successful, and in spring 1956, the corporation was rapidly running out of working capital. While the company was temporarily saved through a deal with Curtiss-Wright, Packard, with all its tradition, magnificence, and newfound potential, was unceremoniously jettisoned—surely one of the saddest days in American automotive history.

Teague's last lamentable duty at Packard was to graft some marque identity onto a Studebaker President Classic shell to create a stopgap Clipper for 1957, a task he accomplished with surprising aplomb. The very last Packards, the '58s with their fishmouth grilles and tacked-on fins, were created by Duncan McRae's Studebaker styling staff under tremendous pressure to create something—anything—new within the constraints of what was still the 1953 Studebaker sedan body.

For Packard, the end came quietly on July 25, 1958, in South Bend, Indiana. But the real Packard lay somewhere in the deserted and decaying buildings of East Grand Boulevard in Detroit. As for the Predictor, it survives in the Studebaker Museum, a tormenting reminder not of what could have been, but what, in a more benevolent universe, *should* have been.

1

When John Reinhart's Packard stylists replaced the bulbous "pregnant elephant" look of 1948 with a new design for 1951, no one knew it would be the last all-new car from the grand marque. Even the final Detroit-built Packards of 1956 were modified derivatives of the '51s.

Reinhart's successor as chief stylist, Dick Teague, facelifted the existing bodies for '53 with an updated grille that still had the make's traditional "ox-yoke" across the top bar. Clippers added hardtoplike wrapped rear windows.

Specialty body supplier Henney had a role, too. Its Pan American show car led to the '53 Caribbean convertible. The firm also revived formal sedans and long-wheelbase limousines.

2

Between stints at Ford, stylist Robin Jones worked at Packard, where he sketched these ideas in the early Fifties. **1.** An April '52 proposal for the 1955 Packard. **2.** This bumper/grille ensemble wouldn't be adopted. **3-4.** Customer comments expressed a longing for the Thirties-style vertical Packard grille. Jones toyed with these proposals in an effort to satisfy the requests. **5.** Another prospective '53 facelift, this with side trim that ran from the massive grille. **6.** In a November 1951 drawing, he proposed doing away with the separate-fender look.

4

5

1. A base Packard series contained this ragtop and the Mayfair hardtop in '53. Wheelbase and rear styling were shared with the cheaper Clippers. **2.** Finlike fender trim was new to the Patrician, which topped the '53 senior line. **3.** Richard Arbib's '52 Pan American show car led to the 1953 Caribbean, which sported open wheel wells, a hood scoop, and wire wheels. **4.** Rear-wheel openings were altered on the '54 Caribbean. Two-toning was added, too. **5-6.** High-mount taillights identified '54 Clippers like this Super Panama hardtop.

6

1

2

The market forces that drove Packard to merge with Studebaker in 1954 didn't let up in following years, especially when it became clear that Studebaker was needier than expected. Packard desperately needed to redesign for 1957. Ideas the company had; money it had not.

The Predictor show car of 1956 bore the hallmarks of the design Dick Teague was proposing for the '57 senior Packards. It had a vertical central grille bar with a hint of the classic "ox yoke" at the top, a hardtop roof with a rear pillar that narrowed at its base, and blade fins that rose over vertical taillights in an extension of themes seen on the production '56 Caribbean.

Packard explored buying Lincoln bodies on which to hang the styling, but no deal could be reached. An in-house prototype of the new design—"Black Bess"—also went for naught. The era of the grand Packard was at an end.

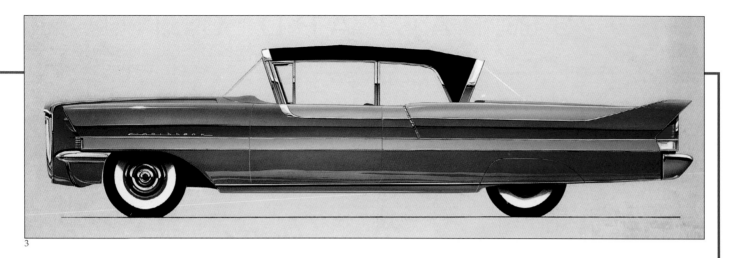

3

4

5

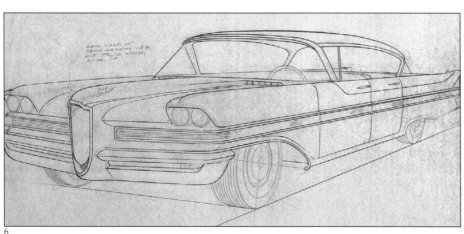

6

1-2. Fred Hudson drew these possible post-'56 Packard updates in 1955 (1) and '56 (2), the latter with influences from the Predictor show car. **3-5.** A convertible and two differently trimmed hardtop coupes proposed for 1958. Drawings 3 and 5 are by Richard Macadam, who led Chrysler Styling in the Seventies. **6.** Back at Ford by the mid Fifties, Robin Jones sketched his take on his former employer's plans.

1

Since coming aboard as Packard's president in 1952, James Nance desperately wanted to separate the lower-priced lines (known as Clippers from '53 on) from the more-prestigious cars. A stillborn plan for 1957 would have clearly done that.

Packard, Clipper, and Studebaker would have shared new inner bodies, but with different sheetmetal. The Clipper was to have looked more like a big Studebaker than a small Packard. In the end, Packard lived out its days in facelifted '56 Studebaker bodies.

2

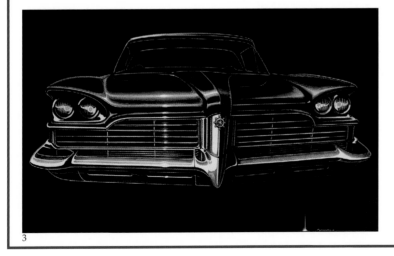

3

4

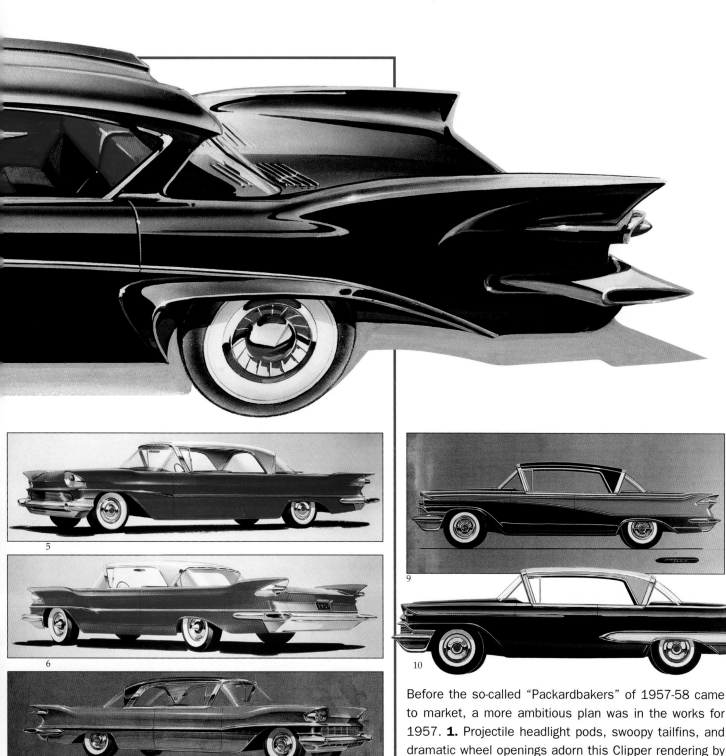

Before the so-called "Packardbakers" of 1957-58 came to market, a more ambitious plan was in the works for 1957. **1.** Projectile headlight pods, swoopy tailfins, and dramatic wheel openings adorn this Clipper rendering by J. Ewart from October '55. **2-4.** Before going on to bigger things at General Motors, Larry Shinoda sketched these Clippers, including an update of the production '56 car (4). **5-6.** The proposed '57 Clipper would have looked nothing like the Packards being considered for the year. **7-8.** Fred Hudson's ideas for a '57 Clipper Custom hardtop and convertible. **9-10.** Side-trim explorations from Shinoda.

1

2

3

Had finances allowed, the 1957-58 Packards might have matched Chrysler Corporation's low, lean look. Instead, the final Packards were tarted-up Studebakers. **1.** The '57 Clipper was designed by Dick Teague to share a bodyshell with the Studebaker President. **2.** A Clipper Country Sedan with emphatic fins and an upright greenhouse. **3.** In '58, the Packard wagon's double-deck fins screamed "Look at me!" Duncan McRae had to update the line as best he could. **4-5.** The 1958 two-door hardtop was Fin City; quad lamps were tacked on up front. **6.** The '58 Hawk made little effort to hide its Stude origins, and was the better for it.

STUDEBAKER
CORPORATION

Studebaker began the Fifties with its most-popular postwar automobile, the 1950-51 bullet-nose cars. Designed under the direction of the inimitable Raymond Loewy, they were something of a departure for Loewy who, though theatrical in manner, was in fact a disciplined arbiter of design. The equally inimitable auto tester, Tom McCahill, thought the '50 Stude looked as if "Preston Tucker had passed through South Bend on a bicycle," McCahill's roundabout way of saying the car resembled the triple-headlight look of the ill-fated rear-engine sedan. The Virgil Exner-designed "which way is it going?" Studebakers of 1947 had established the company as a postwar styling leader, and the bullet-nose jobs were a way of staying there "on the cheap" with carryover bodies. By the time the company celebrated its centennial in 1952, the bullet-nose had given way to a less-pretentious visage.

The following year, Studebaker stunned the competition with what is still considered by many to be the most beautiful American car of the decade. Designed by Loewy staffer Robert Bourke, the Loewy/Bourke two-door coupe and hardtop were exceptional—long, lithe, creations devoid of meaningless ornamentation, with an excellent wheel-to-body ratio, and fronted by a pair of distinctive

slotted grilles. The startled press described the new look as "European." While the coupe and hardtop were mounted on the 120.5-inch Land Cruiser sedan wheelbase, the more prosaic Champion and Commander sedans were set on a 116.5-inch chassis. Some thought the sedans (and later wagons) appeared stunted next to the coupes, although viewed by themselves, the sedans looked decent enough.

Unfortunately, production problems with the coupes limited their initial availability. More ominously, to all those loyalists driving their "bulletproof" bullet-nose Studes, the new beauties looked suspiciously delicate, even feminine. Consequently, by 1954, the bloom was off the rose, hurrying a disillusioned Studebaker management into the supposed safety of a merger with Packard. In an attempt to be closer to "the mainstream," facelifted '55 Studes were slathered with chrome, destroying much of their charm.

Loewy's contract was canceled as Studebaker-Packard President Jim Nance ordered a complete stylistic turnaround. The '56 Studebaker sedans and wagons had a more "Detroit" look, with upright grilles, high hoods and decks, and aggressive two-toning. The Loewy/Burke coupes were transformed into the sports-luxury Hawk series with the addition of a higher, more-prominent central grille up front and fins out back.

Most of this would have disappeared in 1957 had Nance's intentions to have S-P's three marques share a new common bodyshell been achieved. But a lack of ready cash thwarted these plans, destroying Packard in the process and leaving Studebaker to facelift its existing cars for 1957 and '58. Awkward-looking dual headlights and tacky tailfins were a desperate attempt to keep up with Detroit, particularly Chrysler.

Realizing that it could not long continue on this course, Studebaker management, led by president Harold Churchill, decided on an entirely new direction. Hoping to take advantage of the rising popularity of small cars, Churchill ordered his designers and engineers to somehow fashion a new compact out of the '53-vintage body. All the add-ons were chopped away and the remaining shell was effectively cloaked with new sheetmetal to create a fresh-looking automobile of compact proportions with several competitive advantages despite its six-year-old body. Since the '53 sedan had been designed as a full-size car, the new Studebaker's interior dimensions were larger than competitors' like the Rambler American, and both economy sixes and frisky V-8s could be stuffed underhood. What's more, a longer-wheelbase variant existed that could be brought to market should the buying public desire a "bigger" compact car. (This happened in 1961 with the addition of the four-door Cruiser.)

Christened the Lark, the new Stude sported truncated front and rear ends that managed to look attractive despite economies like the use of a bumper that could be used at either end, and dual rather than quad headlights. Studebaker identity was maintained through the use of a Hawk-inspired grille.

That the Lark was accepted by the public as an entirely new car was a fitting and well-earned tribute to Duncan McRae and his staff stylists. Saddled with a six-year-old shell, and faced with limited tooling monies and impossible deadlines, they had conjured up a miracle car that managed to restore Studebaker to health (albeit temporarily). Available in a full range of body styles (including a convertible in '60), the Lark kept production lines in South Bend, Indiana, humming while beleaguered S-P stock shot up in value.

Yet, despite initial success and the happy faces of Studebaker employees, dealers, and customers, Studebaker management looked apprehensively to autumn 1959, when Detroit's Big Three would all launch compact cars that, if successful, could adversely affect the Lark. As it turns out, they had ample reason to be apprehensive.

1

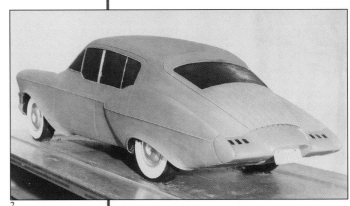

2

Since the late Thirties, famed industrial designer Raymond Loewy had provided designs for Studebaker with one notable exception. As Virgil Exner worked for Loewy and Associates, he began to chafe under his boss's public assumption of all credit for the staff's designs. With help from Studebaker's similarly disenchanted chief engineer, Exner independently developed the all-new 1947-49 "is-it-coming-or-going" car.

Loewy had the last laugh, though. For the 1950 facelift, he wanted an airplane look up front, and staff designer Robert Bourke delivered it. The memorable "bullet-nose" Studebakers of 1950-51 were the result.

When a new design—the Model N—fizzled in the studio, Bourke canned the propeller nose for a predictive sloped-hood facelift for 1952.

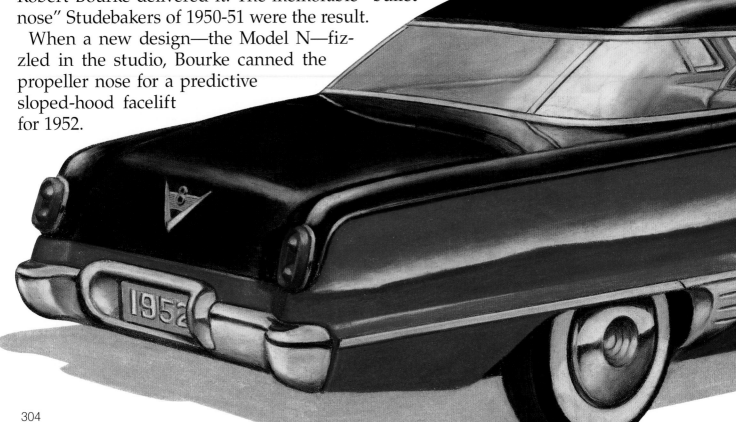

1. This late-Forties small-scale model was an early indicator of the "bullet-nose" look that would distinctively identify Studebakers in 1950 and '51. Its finned fanjet beak might have been more industrial looking than the more-streamlined "propeller spinner" detail ultimately selected for production, but it could have served as an avant-garde symbol of the jet age that was coming to aviation. **2.** The model also featured a fastback roof then so much in vogue, but with a twist: a hatchback deck. **3-4.** A four-door-sedan clay made as an alternative to the Model N, the proposed all-new 1952 Studebaker that was ultimately canceled. **5.** A two-door sedan model from about the same time with different bodyside detailing. **6.** A clay model of a coupe related to the sedan in pictures 3 and 4 was also worked up. The clay continued the unique Starlight roof Studebaker used in the 1947-52 period. This modern artist's conception suggests how the coupe might have looked if it had been approved for production.

1

2

3

4

306

5

6

1-3. The 1950 Commander as convertible, Land Cruiser four-door sedan, and Starlight coupe with Bob Bourke's "bullet-nose" facelift of the 1947-49 bodies. 4. A '51 Champion two-door sedan with bigger, brighter grillework and an add-on bumper bar. Part of the "bullet" surround was now body color. 5. Hardtop styling came to Studebaker for 1952. This Commander Starliner has a 232-cid V-8 under its sloped hood. The firm marked its centennial in '52. 6. A '52 Commander sedan. Note the hooded taillights. 7. Workaday Champion with the new divided grille.

7

1

2

5

8

9

In late 1950, during the ultimately doomed effort to design the Model N, Raymond Loewy decided he wanted a show car. And he wanted it now. Loewy gave four teams of his stylists 10 days to come up with something. The winning design was a coupe from Bob Bourke that was so striking that Studebaker couldn't resist putting a version of it into production for 1953.

The Starliner hardtops and Starlight coupes were built on the long 120.5-inch wheelbase intended for the Land Cruiser sedan. A low hood sloped to a discreet twin-slit grille. Chrome body trim was held to a minimum (at least until '55), giving the cars a somewhat European look. Standard sedans and wagons used this styling on a shorter chassis, but not as successfully as on the coupes.

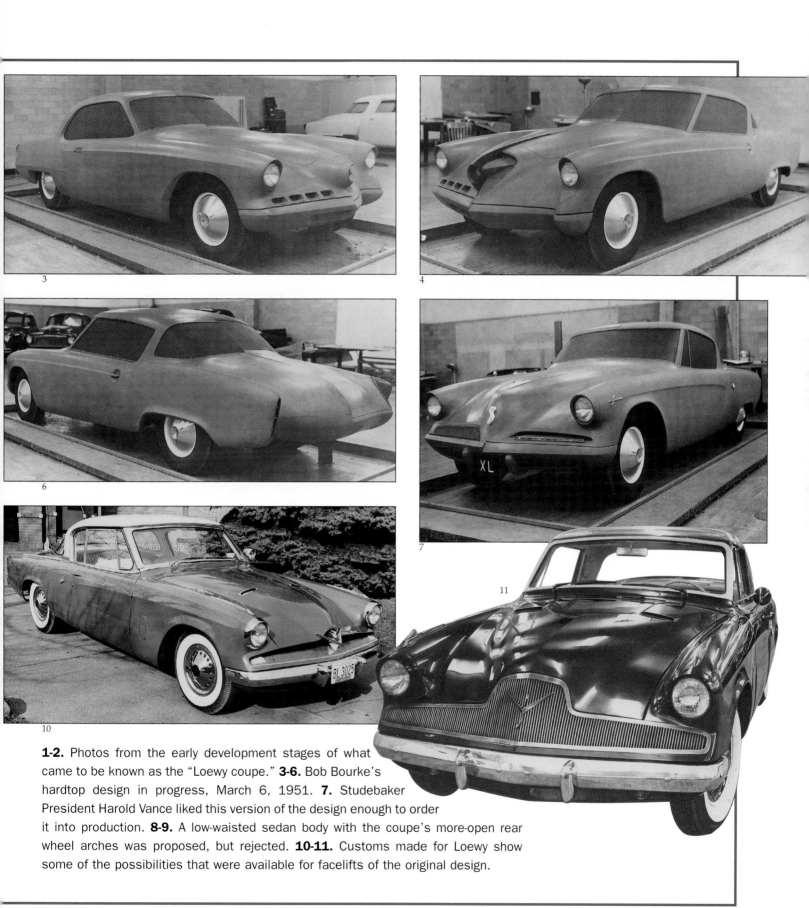

1-2. Photos from the early development stages of what came to be known as the "Loewy coupe." **3-6.** Bob Bourke's hardtop design in progress, March 6, 1951. **7.** Studebaker President Harold Vance liked this version of the design enough to order it into production. **8-9.** A low-waisted sedan body with the coupe's more-open rear wheel arches was proposed, but rejected. **10-11.** Customs made for Loewy show some of the possibilities that were available for facelifts of the original design.

1-3. Stude's 1953 Commander (shown) and Champion coupes came pillared or pillarless. Bob Bourke's design was at once tasteful and ultramodern; an unusual *Time* magazine cover story described the car as "Revolutionary. Spectacular. Beautiful." A production screw up (early front sheetmetal was misaligned), Stude's incorrect assumption that the sedans would outsell the coupes, and a Ford-GM price war hurt the coupe's sales chances. **4.** Vertical grille pieces were added for '54, as seen on this Commander Starlight coupe. **5.** A Conestoga wagon based on sedan tooling arrived for 1954; this is a '55. **6.** Originally a show model, the rakish President Speedster saw limited production for '55. Note the exclusive "tri-level" paint and wide chrome band over the rear portion of the roof.

4

5

6

1

The 1957 and '58 Studebakers weren't supposed to be facelifted '56s. In fact, the 1956 model was intended as little more than a holding action until Studebaker-Packard President James Nance could get his envisioned Packard/Clipper/Studebaker body-sharing program running for 1957. Fate had other ideas, however.

With Loewy's costly contract near its end, S-P opened up the '56 styling derby. Freelance designer Vince Gardner put a new face and tail onto 1953-55 sedan and wagon bodies. Duncan McRae modified the look for 1957 and '58.

2

1-2. The final Loewy-group proposal for a Fifties Studebaker included this '57 hardtop coupe with a grille reminiscent of that on the new Hawk sports coupe, a trendy wrap-around windshield, and strips of taillight that clung to the fender edges. In picture 1, Bob Bourke, chief stylist for Raymond Loewy at Studebaker, admires the clay model on November 18, 1954. **3-5.** A four-door variant with a different grille and added brightwork. **6.** Had S-P management been able to fund all-new bodies, this Duncan McRae design could have been the '58 Studebaker. Packard's Clipper would have shared basic styling.

1. In 1956, the '53-vintage coupe design was transformed into the sporty Hawk. Flaring fins and a supercharged Stude V-8 were new on '57 Golden Hawks. 2. The '57 Silver Hawk was offered with a choice of engines. The ribbed decklid seemed superfluous. 3. Stude didn't offer a four-door wagon until 1957, and even then only with a V-8, like this top-line Broadmoor. 4. The 1958 President with revived hardtop styling and quad headlights in afterthought pods. 5. A modestly trimmed four-door '58 Champion. 6. Though plain, the Scotsman sold in recessionary '58.

4

5

6

WILLYS-OVERLAND COMPANY

For Willys-Overland, salvation in the Fifties was rooted in the indomitable Jeep despite an ambitious, but unsuccessful, return to the passenger-car business.

Through a fortuitous combination of deft maneuvering and sheer luck, Willys-Overland had managed to secure the manufacturing and trademark rights to the jack-of-all-trades Jeep. In fact, production of the battle-tested little 4×4 (and Jeep-inspired derivatives) so consumed the company that reentry into the conventional passenger-car business was temporarily set aside, despite word of a new Brooks Stevens-styled sedan. Though a few prototypes were built, the design was dated. In addition, W-O President Ward Canaday never liked it, sealing its fate.

Former Packard engineer Clyde Paton had patented some ideas on light-car design, and tried to peddle his concept at Willys. Finally, in 1950, Canaday authorized the project with the talented Phil Wright as stylist. Wright had had a successful career in automobile design in the prewar years, particularly with his trend-setting 1933 Pierce Silver Arrow and—thanks to his employment with Briggs Body Manufacturing—the 1935 Ford and Chrysler/DeSoto Airstreams.

Of course, the styling architecture of postwar cars was entirely different from that of the classic era. Beginning with the first Kaiser-Frazer cars, fenders disappeared, subsumed into the flush sides of the new "envelope" bodies. Not many of the classic-era designers were capable of making the adjustment, two notable exceptions being Kaiser-Frazer designer Howard Darrin and Wright.

Introduced in 1952, the Aero-Willys was an attractive, clean-looking design, with high fenders and a flush hood, simple horizontal-bar grille, and a straightforward bodyside trim strip. The only trace of trickery was the hop-up on the rear quarters at the taillights.

Engineering was rock solid, thanks to Paton, and body and frame were combined to form a rigid structure. Bodies were fabricated by longtime body builder Murray. All in all, the Aero-Willys was a real contender. Sales were respectable for awhile, then fell of, especially after the Kaisers took over in 1953. One problem was that the car was smaller than comparable Fords and Chevys, yet the asking price was hundreds more.

In 1955, the car was refreshed with bodyside two-toning and Kaiser-inspired grillework, and then, regrettably, allowed to go out of production as Henry and Edgar Kaiser abandoned automobile assembly at Toledo. Yet the Willys car survived. The dies were shipped to Willys-Overland of Brazil, where the car stayed in production for years.

Had Willys-Overland remained independent, the Willys car would have probably remained in production at Toledo awhile longer. Both Darrin and former K-F designer Buzz Grisinger were each busily working on major facelifts for 1956. But each of their efforts was stillborn as Willys concentrated on the Jeep and whatever variants of it looked promising.

1

H aving resumed motor-vehicle production after World War II with a line of Jeep-derived products, Willys was ready to try a more-conventional car by the early Fifties. It arrived for 1952 as the Aero, a 108-inch-wheelbase compact presented to the company by independent engineer Clyde Paton, with some styling input by Phil Wright, of Pierce Silver Arrow fame.

Willys, which merged with Kaiser in '53, had hoped to substantially update the Aero's looks for 1955 or '56. Buzz Grisinger—ex of Kaiser—and consulting partner Rhys Miller developed an ambitious new face for the car. But Kaiser-Willys could not afford to put it into production, and the final Willys wore a simpler facelift.

2

3

4

5

1. The Buzz Grisinger/Rhys Miller proposal for a 1955 or '56 Willys. The consulting team's distinctive grille would have made the squarish Aero look lower and wider. The rear fenders would have been smoothed out, too. In the end, though, Kaiser-Willys couldn't afford to produce the redesign. **2-5.** Bob Gurr, who was recruited to provide Kaiser styling ideas for Grisinger and Miller, was also put to work on prospective 1955 Willys concepts.

Willys's tidy and handsome Aero series sold reasonably well from its inception in 1952 through the '53 model year. Some 1954 Aeros appeared under the stewardship of a new owner, Kaiser, which saw production plummet by nearly 75 percent, to 11,717. **1.** With an ambitious restyle for '55 out of the question, Kaiser designers Buzz Grisinger and Herb Weissinger tweaked the Ace, Custom, and Bermuda (the Aero name had been dropped) with a reworked grille featuring a panel of concave vertical teeth, and faintly unorthodox "Z-line" bodyside trim. **2.** "Finlet" fendertops were capped with shapely, high-riding taillights that incorporated pointed back-up lamps. The Bermuda hardtop looked as good as most of its contemporaries, but for '55, Kaiser-Willys moved only about 6000 Willys cars.

1

2

INDEX